Campbell's
MICROWAVE
COOKBOOK

CAMPBELL MICROWAVE INSTITUTE

BEEKMAN HOUSE
New York

This edition was prepared by the Publications Center and the Campbell Microwave Institute, Campbell Soup Company, Campbell Place, Camden, NJ 08103-1799.

Editors: Julia Malloy, Flora E. Szatkowski
Recipe Coordinators: Barbara A. Lynch, Dorcas B. Reilly
Home Economists: Jennifer L. Andersen, Elaine M. Gagliardi, Rose M. Smith-Brydon
Photographers: William R. Houssell, Nancy B. Principato, Maggie Wochele
Art Director: Warren Neal
Photo Coordinator: Jacqueline Finch
Food Stylists: Elizabeth J. Barlow, Maria J. Soriano
Accessories Stylist: Kathryn B. Foden

CAMPBELL MICROWAVE INSTITUTE
Susan Whittier, Co-Director—Marketing
Warren Widicus, Ph.D., Co-Director—Technical
Peter Dakich, Media Services
Paul D. Garwood, Microwave Packaging Development
Vince Hatton, Plastic Container Development
Stan H. Kwis, Microwave Product Development
Henry K. Leung, Ph.D., Microwave Product Development
Barbara A. Lynch, Creative Food Center
Kevin J. Murphy, Sales Planning
John P. O'Meara, Microwave Technology
William P. Piszek, Marketing Research
Charles E. Schick, Promotions
Frederick E. Simon, Ph.D., Microwave Packaging Research
Mary S. Toporek, Communications

On the front cover: Glazed Stuffed Cornish Hens (see page 60).
On the back cover from top to bottom: Cheesecake Pie (see page 178), Orange-Ginger Fish (see page 80), Pasta with Vegetables (see page 142).

Library of Congress Catalog Card Number: 87-63422

ISBN: 0-517-65522-5

This edition published by:
Beekman House
Distributed by Crown Publishers, Inc.
225 Park Avenue South
New York, New York 10003

Printed and bound in Yugoslavia by Zrinski

h g f e d c b a

Contents

Campbell, Your Microwave Oven and You

The microwave oven has revolutionized the way we cook and, to some extent, the way we live. The fast-cooking, fast-cleanup qualities of microwave cooking fit right into the nonstop lifestyles of today's busy men and women. In little more than two decades, the microwave oven has earned a place in a majority of American homes.

The resulting cooking revolution presents an exciting challenge. Whether you've cooked with a microwave oven for a few weeks or a few years, you'll probably agree that there's more to learn every day. There are new food products and packages, cookware and utensils to discover. The makers of paper towels, plastic wrap and foil are coming out with new ways to use these kitchen aids for cooking. And the food products you've relied upon for years offer microwave heating directions so you can use them with confidence.

What makes microwave cooking so special? First, of course, is the speed with which it heats and cooks food. Before the microwave oven, who ever dreamed that a five-minute baked potato was possible! Or that hamburger could be thawed in less time than it takes to fire up a grill!

Your microwave oven is second only to your dishwasher in helping you clean up, too. You can cook and serve frozen dinners in their throwaway containers and heat soup in its serving bowl. Because cooking utensils stay relatively cool, food doesn't stick to them as readily as in conventional cooking methods.

Microwave cooking tends to be low-fat cooking, good for calorie-watchers. Because microwave cooking is like steaming, it's also a particularly good way to prepare vegetables and fish and to reheat casseroles and other foods you want to remain moist.

Finally, as you'll learn from this book and your own experience, the microwave oven provides a host of new shortcuts and problem solvers, such as melting butter, thawing frozen foods and reheating leftovers.

Microwave cooking is not magic. It doesn't cook everything more quickly than other methods, nor is it always more convenient. But there are foods that microwave ovens cook better, faster or more efficiently, and these are the focus of this book.

Campbell's family of products teams up with your microwave oven to help you make the most of every minute you spend in the kitchen. The rich, full flavors of Campbell's soups, Swanson broths, Prego spaghetti sauces and Franco-American gravies put homemade taste into your quick meals. Swanson frozen chicken, dinners and entrées; Le Menu and LightStyle dinners, Great Starts frozen breakfasts and Mrs. Paul's frozen fish and vegetables help you skip major cooking steps. Pepperidge Farm baked goods, "V8" vegetable juice and Vlasic pickles work both as recipe ingredients and accompaniments to fine meals.

There is one message we'd most like you to take away from this book: *Microwave cooking is simply another way to cook.* Your microwave oven will never replace all your other cooking appliances, but, as you gain experience, you'll discover it's the best appliance for many cooking steps and a great friend to busy people.

We asked a panel of experienced microwave oven owners what advice they would like to pass on to others. Their advice was the same as ours: *Use it!* The more you do, the more you'll learn about the benefits of microwave cooking.

We hope this book will help you do just that.

How Your Microwave Oven Works

Inside your microwave oven is a magnetron tube that converts electrical energy into microwave energy. The microwave energy is directed into the oven and reflects off the walls and floor until it is absorbed by food, making the food hot. Because microwaves work directly on the food, they don't waste energy heating the air or the food's container; that's why microwaves heat many foods more quickly and efficiently than other cooking methods do.

If you've ever used a microwave oven other than your own, you know how different they can be—with different controls on the outside, larger or smaller oven cavities, maybe a shelf or turntable inside.

Microwave ovens also vary greatly in how they work. Some have energy entering the oven from the top, some from the bottom, some from the sides and some from more than one direction. Some cook more quickly, some more slowly; some heat more evenly, while others have hot spots where food tends to cook first.

The best way to learn how your own appliance works is to read the manual that came with it, then experiment with a variety of foods. You'll learn where the hot spots are in your oven and whether it consistently cooks foods more quickly or more slowly than average.

What Microwave Ovens Do Best

Because the results of microwave cooking are similar to those of steam cooking, the microwave oven works best on foods you might otherwise steam. High moisture foods such as vegetables and fruits are naturals, as are tender fish and chicken. Meats that benefit from the moist heat of braising also work well.

Cakes and breads can be cooked in a microwave oven; however, the results may disappoint you because the short cooking time and moist heat will not produce conventional texture and browning.

Foods that require rehydrating, such as rice, pasta and dried beans can be microwaved, but will require about the same amount of time as conventional cooking. Because these foods have a tendency to boil over in the microwave oven, you may prefer to cook them conventionally.

Foods that should have a crisp, brown crust do not work in the microwave oven without special equipment. Very large quantities of liquids may require more time in the microwave oven than on the range and deep-fat frying should not be attempted in a microwave oven.

Factors That Affect Microwave Cooking

Don't get the idea that you must forget everything you know about cooking. Microwave cooking isn't really so different from traditional cooking, and the factors that affect microwave cooking time are similar to those that affect any cooking method.

For example, microwave cooking time is greatly affected by the **quantity** of food in the oven. In your microwave oven, a single cup of water boils nearly twice as fast as 2 cups. The same is true of water in a kettle on the stove. Keep in mind that this means additional time is needed for the extra potato or onion you add to a recipe or the extra-large chicken breasts you bought.

The **size** of the pieces of food also affects the time: small cubes of potato cook more quickly and evenly than large ones; thinner slices cook more quickly than thick ones.

Appropriate **arrangement** of the food in your microwave oven can help the food cook better. Arrangements with thicker, slower-cooking pieces toward the outside edge usually work best. The food in the center is generally the last to cook. The same principle applies to the **shapes** of foods such as cakes and casseroles. Round or ring shapes work best; corners of square foods may cook too quickly.

Variations in the **starting temperature of a food** can change its cooking time. You know the same is true of conventional cooking, if you've ever tried to cook a frozen roast; however, shorter microwave cooking times make the difference more apparent.

The **composition of a food** can affect the way it heats. Foods with higher concentrations of fat, sugar or salt attract microwaves more readily than those with lower concentrations.

Using the **proper utensil** makes a difference, too. Be sure to use a dish large enough to allow for boiling and stirring. Think about how full you'd want a saucepan, not an oven-going casserole. Food tends to cook more evenly in round dishes than ones with corners, and food spread out in a shallow dish will cook faster than the same food placed in a narrow, deep dish.

Microwave ovens vary (by manufacturer, model and even by unit) in how quickly and evenly they cook. Your microwave oven may have a **wave pattern** that requires you to stir or rotate foods more often than recipes suggest, or it may cook so evenly that you can skip some of these directions—experience with your oven can teach you that.

In some microwave ovens, **elevating** the food on an inverted microwave-safe pie plate may bring it into a more favorable wave pattern, especially for baked goods and quiches.

Wattage

One thing you should know about your microwave oven is its **wattage**. Wattage is a good indicator of how fast your oven will cook. Our recipes have been tested in 650- to 700-watt microwave ovens. These are among the fastest cooking microwave ovens. Many of the smaller units being sold today are rated lower—as low as 350 watts—and therefore cook more slowly. If you have one of these, you will probably need to add more time to each step of every recipe.

The actual wattage output of your microwave oven may vary with other conditions, too. For example, when electrical demand is high (as in the summer when air conditioners are operating), voltage entering the house may be lower than normal, causing your microwave oven to operate less efficiently. Even operating several appliances at once in your own home can cause a decrease in efficiency.

You may find the wattage rating for your microwave oven listed in its use-and-care guide, or it may be printed somewhere on the appliance. If you can't find it, you can perform a simple test to approximate the wattage (see box below) or contact the manufacturer.

Wattage Test

Here's a quick test you can use to get an idea of the wattage output of your microwave oven.

Combine 1 cup water with ice in a 2-cup measure or other utensil. Stir 2 minutes or until ice stops melting and water is very cold. Remove ice; pour 1 cup of the cold water into a 1-cup glass measure. Microwave, uncovered, on HIGH until water begins to boil.

If water boils in less than 3½ minutes, your microwave oven is producing 600 to 700 watts of energy on HIGH. If it takes 3½ to 4½ minutes to boil, wattage output is 500 to 600 watts. If the heating time is greater than 4½ minutes, wattage output is less than 500 watts.

This test will give you an approximation of wattage output; however, your microwave oven's efficiency may vary depending on the quantity and kind of food being cooked.

Microwave Cooking Know-How

To use your microwave oven most effectively, you should be familiar with some pointers that will make these and other microwave cooking recipes the best they can be.

Power Settings

Most of today's microwave ovens have a range of power settings to choose from, and they vary from oven to oven, even within the same brand. Settings may have names such as "defrost," "simmer" or "medium" or they may be indicated by numbers from 1 to 10. For power settings other than HIGH, the microwave power cycles on and off, controlling the total amount of microwave energy being sent to the food. Higher power settings are used for faster cooking, while lower settings help cook food more slowly and evenly.

Two different power settings are used in these recipes. **HIGH** power is called for most often. On HIGH, the microwave oven is operating at full power the entire time it is on. At **50% power**, the microwave energy cycles on and off at equal intervals to provide slower cooking. Your oven may have other names for these settings, so consult your use-and-care manual or contact the manufacturer for more information.

If your microwave oven has a low wattage rating, you may wish to use a higher setting (such as 60% or 70%) when we call for 50% power to compensate for the lower wattage.

Containers

You probably know that metal cooking dishes are rarely used in the microwave oven because they reflect the waves away from the food, slowing the cooking. Metal, if improperly used, may also cause arcing (sparks). The metallic gold or silver trim on some china may arc and discolor, so these dishes should also be avoided. Your microwave oven manual will explain what, if any, metal may be used in your particular oven. If you do use metal, be sure to use only small amounts and to keep it away from the sides and floor of the oven, which may be metal.

There are many glass and ceramic utensils on the market today made especially for microwave cooking, but not all kinds of glassware and china are suitable for microwave oven use. To test whether a container is microwavable, place it in your microwave oven alongside a cup of cold tap water. Microwave on HIGH 1 minute. If the water is warm and the container is cool, the container may be used. If the container is warm or has warm spots, it is not microwavable. (This test is not suitable for plastic containers.)

Many plastics are ideal for microwave cooking, and today's stores are full of plastics that have been developed especially for microwave oven use. There are other plastics that are unsuitable for microwaving—some because they can melt from the heat of the food, others because they absorb microwaves. To be certain, use only plastics that the manufacturer says are microwave-safe.

Paper plates and paper towels may be used for some microwave cooking. Avoid using paper with dyes that might leach into the food. Recycled paper products are not recommended because they may contain materials that could ignite in your microwave oven.

There are specialty items that you may wish to buy for microwave cooking. For example, browning trays can give meats a browned appearance and flavor, microwave meat racks hold bacon and other meats above their drippings, and some microwave muffin pans have perforated bottoms that allow steam to escape.

How to Tell the Size of a Casserole or Baking Dish

If you're not sure how much your casseroles hold, there's a simple way to determine their volume. Simply fill the dish with a measured amount of water. The quantity of water needed to fill the dish to the rim is its volume.

For baking dishes, the measurements given are the dish's length and width, measured from the inside edges.

Covers

Covering a food holds in steam to keep it moist, distributes the heat more evenly and contains spatters.

Close-fitting lids and plastic wrap can be used interchangeably for the tightest covers. Choose a lid that is made of a microwave-safe material and fits the dish snugly.

Plastic wrap is especially versatile because it will fit any size or shape of dish. Look for a brand that claims to be microwavable; some others may melt if they touch hot food. When you use plastic wrap, fold back one corner of the wrap to provide a vent for the excess steam, or the wrap may split.

Always remove a tight cover carefully, away from your face; even though the dish may seem cool, steam built up under the cover can be very hot and dangerous.

When you want to keep a minimum of steam in the dish, cover the food loosely with waxed paper to keep food moist and control spatters. A paper towel cover can absorb grease or excess moisture; again, use paper towels that are free of dyes and have not been made from recycled products.

Some foods, such as cakes and foods with a crumb coating, are cooked uncovered to promote a dry, not soggy surface.

Stirring, Rotating and Rearranging

To cook food more evenly, recipes often call for stirring, rotating or rearranging the food.

Stirring is most effective in distributing the heat; just stir the food with a spoon to distribute the heat throughout the dish.

Foods that cannot be stirred, such as fish and layered casseroles, should be **rotated.** Rotate a dish by turning it in a counterclockwise or clockwise motion; one-quarter (90°) turns are most effective, but one-half (180°) turns can be used when a dish is longer than the oven is wide.

Rearrange when there are several pieces of food or dishes in the oven. When rearranging, turn foods so that they are in a different position in the oven and the outside pieces are toward the inside. If possible, turn foods over so that bottoms are on the top.

Doneness and Standing Time

Some recipes call for standing time to complete cooking and to allow the heat to distribute evenly throughout the food. For standing, simply place the food directly on a flat surface such as a countertop or cutting board. Better yet, leave the dish in the microwave oven with the power off; do not use a cooling rack.

It is easy to overcook foods in a microwave oven, so if the food seems nearly done, let it complete its standing time, then check for doneness, adding more cooking time in short intervals as needed.

Modifying Microwave Recipes

You may be so used to doubling or halving conventional recipes that you don't think about it. Microwave recipes need more consideration.

When doubling a microwave recipe, be sure the dish size is adequate. You may not want to double the liquid, because evaporation is slower than in conventional cooking. You'll definitely need more cooking time; start with about 50% more time, then check for doneness.

When you halve a recipe, keep the same size dish, but reduce the cooking time. Start with half of the full recipe time; check often.

If you alter a recipe, you can affect the cooking time. See *Factors That Affect Microwave Cooking* on page 6 for more information.

Microwave Cooking Times

Cooking times for recipes depend on your oven wattage and other factors. The recipe times given in this book are the *minimum cooking times* needed in 650- to 700-watt ovens. Your oven may consistently require more time than suggested, especially if you have a 400- to 500-watt oven. (See page 8 for more information on wattage.) For the best indicator of cooking time, follow the recipe descriptions of how the food should look when done.

Caring for Your Microwave Oven

Your microwave oven needs some care. Keep it clean and do not obstruct any vents. Place it on a stable surface where it will not be jarred.

For best results, plug your oven into its own grounded circuit. Be aware that any time several appliances are on the same electrical circuit, the combination may overload the circuit.

Never operate your microwave oven when empty. If you have children who may turn it on, keep a cup of water inside to absorb microwaves.

Microwave ovens are very safe; however, if yours has been damaged in some way, microwave leakage may occur. In such a case, have it checked by a microwave service professional.

Campbell Microwave Institute

The Campbell Microwave Institute (CMI) was established in 1986 to promote microwave cooking, both by improving the quality of microwavable foods and by teaching consumers to make the most of their microwave ovens. It's a big task, but it's one that our team of scientists, home economists and other specialists is well-qualified to tackle.

This book fulfills a small part of our mission. It will help take the mystery out of microwave cooking for you and show you how to use your microwave oven in many different ways every day.

In other areas of consumer education and product development, CMI has already made outstanding progress. Here are a few examples of our work:

- Swanson dinners and entrées, Le Menu dinners, Mrs. Paul's entrées and Great Starts breakfasts are now packaged in microwavable plastic or paperboard containers. In addition, Pepperidge Farm uses a wonderful new container that makes a crispy croissant pizza in the microwave oven.

- Microwave cooking directions are included on most of our packaging, including Campbell's soups and beans, Franco-American pastas and gravies and Prego spaghetti sauces, as well as the frozen foods mentioned above.

- We've developed award-winning microwavable packaging in our recently opened Campbell Plastics Center, packages that will simplify your daily cooking chores and improve the results of foods prepared in the microwave oven.

- Working on research to further the scientific knowledge of how food and packaging materials respond to microwave energy, we have shared findings with the microwave industry and media representatives.

- We've made our team of experts available to newspapers, magazines and other news media to keep them abreast of the latest developments in this fast-changing subject area, so they can transmit this information to you.

Whether you're a microwave cooking novice or a pro, there is much to learn. Let us know if you have any insights to share or questions we can answer, and we will continue to be the microwave cooking resource that meets the needs of home cooks and professionals.

Appetizers

Party Scramble

½ cup butter or margarine, cut up
1 pouch Campbell's Onion Soup and Recipe Mix
1 cup bite-size wheat cereal squares
1 cup bite-size corn cereal squares
1 bag (6 ounces) Pepperidge Farm Cheddar Cheese
    Goldfish Crackers
1 bag (5½ ounces) Pepperidge Farm Pretzel Goldfish
    Crackers
2 cups unsalted peanuts

1. Place butter in 2-cup glass measure. Cover; microwave on HIGH 45 seconds or until melted. Stir in soup mix.

2. In 4-quart microwave-safe bowl, combine remaining ingredients. Pour butter mixture over cracker mixture; toss to coat well. Microwave, uncovered, on HIGH 5 minutes or until hot, stirring twice during heating.

3. Cool. Store mixture in airtight container. Makes about 10 cups.

PARTY SCRAMBLE ▶

Onion-Buttered Popcorn

If you wish to use one of the microwavable popcorn products on the market, buy the unsalted variety.

½ cup butter or margarine, cut up
1 pouch Campbell's Onion Soup and Recipe Mix
4 quarts popped popcorn

1. Place butter in 4-cup glass measure. Cover; microwave on HIGH 45 seconds or until melted. Stir in soup mix.

2. Place popcorn in very large bowl. Pour butter mixture over popcorn. Toss until evenly distributed. Makes 16 cups or 8 servings.

Note: This butter and onion soup mixture is also delicious served on bread, potatoes, vegetables and grilled meats.

TIP To melt butter, place 2 tablespoons butter in glass measure. Cover; microwave on HIGH 30 seconds.

Hot Chili Dip

2 tablespoons butter or margarine
½ cup chopped green pepper
¼ cup chopped onion
2 teaspoons chili powder
1 can (19½ ounces) Campbell's Chunky Chili Beef Soup
1 cup shredded Cheddar cheese (4 ounces)
¼ cup sliced pitted ripe olives for garnish
¼ cup sliced green onions for garnish

1. In 1½-quart microwave-safe casserole, combine butter, green pepper, onion and chili powder. Cover with lid; microwave on HIGH 3 minutes or until vegetables are tender, stirring once during cooking.

2. Stir in soup. Cover; microwave on HIGH 4 minutes or until hot and bubbling, stirring once during cooking.

3. Pour into microwave-safe serving dish. Sprinkle with cheese. Microwave, uncovered, on HIGH 1 minute or until cheese is melted. Sprinkle with olives and green onions. Serve with tortilla chips for dipping. Makes about 2½ cups.

Guacamole-Chili Dip

1 medium avocado, peeled, seeded and cut up
1 tablespoon lemon juice
1 tablespoon finely chopped onion
1 small clove garlic, minced
¼ teaspoon salt
⅛ teaspoon hot pepper sauce
½ pound ground beef
½ cup chopped onion
1 can (11¼ ounces) Campbell's Condensed Chili Beef
    Soup
1 cup shredded Cheddar cheese (4 ounces)
1 cup chopped lettuce
1 medium tomato, chopped

1. To prepare guacamole: In covered blender or food processor, combine first 6 ingredients; blend until smooth. Cover and set aside.

2. Crumble beef into 1½-quart microwave-safe casserole. Add ½ cup onion. Cover with lid; microwave on HIGH 3 minutes or until meat is no longer pink, stirring once to break up meat. Spoon off fat.

3. Stir in soup until well blended. Spread on 10-inch microwave-safe platter. Sprinkle with cheese. Microwave, uncovered, on HIGH 2 minutes or until cheese is melted, rotating dish once during cooking.

4. Sprinkle lettuce and tomato over cheese; spoon guacamole in center. Serve with tortilla chips for dipping. Makes 8 appetizer servings.

Note: Serve this hearty dip as a main dish. In step 3, divide soup mixture into four 10-ounce casseroles. Sprinkle with cheese. Microwave, uncovered, on HIGH 3 minutes or until cheese is nearly melted. Divide remaining ingredients among dishes.

TIP To make quick nachos: In 1-quart microwave-safe casserole, stir together 1 can (11 ounces) Campbell's Condensed Nacho Cheese Soup/Dip and ¼ cup milk. Cover with lid; microwave on HIGH 2½ minutes or until hot and bubbling. Arrange 4 cups tortilla chips on a platter. Pour hot soup mixture over chips and garnish with jalapeño peppers, chopped avocado, sliced olives and sliced green onions if desired.

Hot Shrimp Dip

If you prefer, simply serve this easy dip in an attractive 2-cup bowl and omit the bread; use chips or fresh vegetables for dippers.

1 package (8 ounces) cream cheese, cut up
1 can (10¾ ounces) Campbell's Condensed Cream of
  Shrimp Soup
¼ cup finely chopped onion
1 teaspoon prepared horseradish
1 round loaf (10 inches) Italian bread

1. Place cream cheese in 1½-quart microwave-safe casserole. Microwave, uncovered, on HIGH 1 minute or until very soft. Beat in soup until smooth.

2. Stir in onion and horseradish. Cover; microwave on HIGH 4 minutes or until hot and bubbling, stirring once during cooking.

3. Meanwhile, slice off top of bread loaf; hollow out center of bread, leaving 1-inch-thick shell. Cut top and center of bread into cubes for dipping; set aside.

4. Place bread shell on microwave-safe plate; spoon hot soup mixture into shell. Microwave, uncovered, on HIGH 30 seconds or until bread is just warm. Serve with bread cubes for dipping. Makes about 2 cups dip.

Swiss Fondue

1 can (11 ounces) Campbell's Condensed Cheddar
  Cheese Soup/Sauce
2 cups shredded Swiss cheese (8 ounces)
½ cup water or beer
¼ teaspoon Worcestershire sauce
½ teaspoon prepared mustard
⅛ teaspoon hot pepper sauce
  Cubed French bread for dipping

1. In 2-quart microwave-safe casserole, stir soup until smooth; stir in cheese, water, Worcestershire, mustard and hot pepper sauce.

2. Microwave, uncovered, on HIGH 5 minutes or until cheese is melted, stirring twice during cooking. Serve with bread cubes for dipping. Makes about 2 cups.

Appetizer Ham Balls

¾ pound ground ham
¾ pound ground pork
½ cup seasoned fine dry bread crumbs
  1 egg
  1 can (10¾ ounces) Campbell's Condensed Tomato Soup
½ cup packed brown sugar
¼ cup vinegar
½ teaspoon dry mustard

1. In medium bowl, thoroughly mix ham, pork, bread crumbs and egg. Shape mixture into 1-inch meatballs. Arrange in single layer in 12- by 8-inch microwave-safe baking dish. Cover with vented plastic wrap; microwave on HIGH 8 minutes or until meatballs are firm, rearranging meatballs once during cooking. Spoon off fat. Let stand, covered, while preparing sauce.

2. In 4-cup glass measure, combine soup, sugar, vinegar and mustard. Microwave, uncovered, on HIGH 3 minutes or until bubbling, stirring once during cooking.

3. Pour sauce over meatballs. Cover; microwave on HIGH 3 minutes or until heated through. Makes about 45 meatballs.

Note: If you don't see ground ham in your supermarket, ask the butcher to grind it for you, or finely chop cubed cooked ham in a food processor.

Pizza Fondue

½ cup finely chopped pepperoni
  1 sweet red or green pepper, chopped
  4 ounces cream cheese, cut into cubes
⅓ cup grated Parmesan cheese
  1 jar (15½ ounces) Prego Spaghetti Sauce
    Cubed Italian bread for dipping

1. In 1½-quart microwave-safe casserole, combine pepperoni and pepper. Cover with lid; microwave on HIGH 3 minutes or until pepper is tender, stirring once during cooking.

2. Stir in cream cheese and Parmesan until smooth and well blended. Stir in spaghetti sauce. Cover; microwave on HIGH 5 minutes or until hot and bubbling, stirring once during cooking. Serve with bread cubes for dipping. Makes about 3 cups.

Bean Dip

**1 can (16 ounces) Campbell's Pork & Beans in Tomato
Sauce**
**¾ cup shredded Monterey Jack cheese with jalapeño
peppers (3 ounces)**
¼ cup chopped green pepper
¼ cup chopped sweet red pepper
1 tablespoon finely chopped onion
1 or 2 Tortilla Cups* (recipe follows)

1. With fork or potato masher, coarsely mash beans in 1-quart microwave-safe casserole. Stir in cheese, peppers and onion.

2. Cover with lid; microwave on HIGH 3 minutes or until dip is hot and cheese is melted, stirring once during cooking. Spoon into Tortilla Cup; serve with vegetables for dipping. Makes about 2 cups.

Tortilla Cups: For each, brush both sides of 8-inch flour tortilla with melted butter. Place over inverted 2-cup glass measure. Microwave on HIGH 30 seconds. Press tortilla to side of measure. Microwave on HIGH 30 seconds more. Allow to cool on measure.

*Tortilla cup will soften when filled with dip. To prevent this, place custard cup filled with dip inside tortilla cup. Or, make two cups and replace with a freshly filled cup when the first one is empty.

Zesty Smoked Sausages

**1 can (11 ounces) Campbell's Condensed Zesty Tomato
Soup/Sauce**
½ cup orange marmalade or apricot preserves
2 tablespoons vinegar
1 teaspoon dry mustard
**1 pound tiny smoked sausage links or kielbasa, cut into
bite-size pieces**

1. In 2-quart microwave-safe casserole, stir together soup, marmalade, vinegar and mustard until well blended.

2. Stir in sausages. Cover with lid; microwave on HIGH 7 minutes or until hot and bubbling, stirring once during cooking. To serve, spear with cocktail picks. Makes about 30 appetizers.

BEAN DIP ▶

Saucy Meatballs

1 pound lean ground beef
1 pouch Campbell's Onion Soup and Recipe Mix
¼ cup crushed saltines
1 egg
¼ cup water
¼ cup ketchup
2 tablespoons brown sugar
1 tablespoon vinegar
Dash ground allspice

1. In large bowl, thoroughly mix beef, ¼ cup of the soup mix, saltines and egg. Shape mixture into 1-inch meatballs. Arrange in single layer in 12- by 8-inch microwave-safe baking dish.

2. Stir together remaining soup mix, water, ketchup, sugar, vinegar and allspice. Pour over meatballs. Cover with waxed paper; microwave on HIGH 5 minutes or until meat is no longer pink, rearranging meatballs and spooning sauce over meatballs once during cooking. Let stand, covered, 5 minutes. Makes about 30 meatballs.

TIP   Here's an easy way to shape meatballs so they're all the same size for even cooking. On waxed paper, pat meat mixture out to a 1-inch-thick square. With a large knife, cut meat into desired number of squares, then roll each square in your hands to form a meatball.

Bullshot

1 cup "V8" Vegetable Juice
1 cup Swanson Clear Ready to Serve Beef Broth
2 teaspoons lemon juice
¼ teaspoon prepared horseradish

In 4-cup glass measure, stir together all ingredients. Cover with vented plastic wrap; microwave on HIGH 3 minutes or until boiling. Makes about 2 cups or 2 servings.

Smoky Cheddar Ball

    1 teaspoon vegetable oil
    ½ cup finely chopped onion
    ½ cup finely chopped celery
    1 package (3 ounces) cream cheese, cut up
    1 can (11½ ounces) Campbell's Condensed Bean with
        Bacon Soup
 1½ cups shredded Cheddar cheese (6 ounces)
    1 teaspoon Worcestershire sauce
    Chopped fresh parsley

1. In 1-quart microwave-safe casserole, combine oil, onion and celery. Cover with lid; microwave on HIGH 3 minutes or until vegetables are tender. Stir in cream cheese. Microwave, uncovered, on HIGH 30 seconds or until cream cheese is very soft.

2. In large bowl, mash soup with fork. Stir in cream cheese mixture, Cheddar cheese and Worcestershire until well blended. Cover; refrigerate until firm, about 3 hours. Shape into a ball; roll in parsley to coat. Serve with crackers. Makes about 3 cups.

Mushroom Spread

    2 tablespoons butter or margarine
    2 tablespoons sliced green onion
    1 tablespoon all-purpose flour
    1 package (8 ounces) Campbell's Fresh Mushrooms,
        coarsely chopped
    2 tablespoons dry vermouth
    ¼ cup toasted chopped almonds (see Note on page 125)
    2 tablespoons grated Parmesan cheese

1. In 1½-quart microwave-safe casserole, combine butter and onion. Cover with lid; microwave on HIGH 2 minutes or until onion is tender, stirring once during cooking.

2. Stir in flour until smooth. Stir in mushrooms and vermouth. Microwave, uncovered, on HIGH 5 minutes or until mushrooms are tender, stirring once during cooking. Stir in almonds and cheese. Cool slightly.

3. In covered blender or food processor, blend mushroom mixture until finely chopped but not smooth. Pack into bowl or crock. Cover; refrigerate until serving time, at least 4 hours. Serve with crackers. Makes about 1¼ cups.

Country Pâté

The center of this tasty pâté is a surprising mosaic of ham and chicken pieces.

  4 slices bacon
  1 pound ground beef
  ½ pound cooked ham, cut into ¼-inch pieces
  ½ pound raw skinless boneless chicken breast, cut into
      ¼-inch pieces
  2 eggs
  1 pouch Campbell's Onion Soup and Recipe Mix
  2 tablespoons brandy
  ½ teaspoon pepper
  ¼ teaspoon ground nutmeg
    Watercress for garnish
    Cherry tomatoes for garnish

1. Arrange bacon slices ½ inch apart across bottom and up sides of 9- by 5-inch microwave-safe loaf dish; set aside.

2. In medium bowl, thoroughly mix beef, ham, chicken, eggs, soup mix, brandy, pepper and nutmeg. Spoon meat mixture into bacon-lined dish, packing down firmly. Fold ends of bacon over filling.

3. Cover with waxed paper; microwave on HIGH 8 minutes, rotating once during cooking. Carefully pour off fat. Cover; microwave on HIGH 8 minutes or until center is firm, rotating dish twice during cooking. Let stand, covered, 10 minutes. Pour off fat. Invert onto serving plate. Cover; refrigerate until serving time, at least 4 hours.

4. Cut loaf into thin slices. Garnish with watercress and cherry tomatoes. Serve with crackers and mustard. Makes 18 appetizer servings.

Note: If you are using a temperature probe, cook pâté to an internal temperature of 175° to 185°F.

COUNTRY PÂTÉ ▶

Chicken Liver Pâté

**2 packages (8 ounces each) Swanson Frozen Chicken
    Livers**
¼ cup water
1 pouch Campbell's Onion Soup and Recipe Mix
2 slices bacon, chopped
¼ cup butter or margarine, cut up
2 tablespoons brandy
½ teaspoon dry mustard
¼ teaspoon dried thyme leaves, crushed
¼ teaspoon pepper
**   Fresh parsley for garnish**
**   Chopped hard-cooked egg for garnish**

1. Remove frozen livers from boxes but do not remove from pouches. Place in 2-quart microwave-safe casserole. Microwave, uncovered, at 50% power 5 minutes, turning pouches over once during cooking. Let stand 5 minutes. Remove livers from pouches and place in same casserole.

2. Add water, soup mix and bacon. Cover with lid; microwave on HIGH 5 minutes, stirring twice during cooking. Reduce power to 50%. Cover; microwave 4 minutes or until livers are no longer pink, stirring once during cooking.

3. In covered blender or food processor, combine liver mixture, butter, brandy, mustard, thyme and pepper. Blend until smooth.

4. Spoon mixture into 3-cup crock. Cover; refrigerate 4 hours or overnight. Garnish with parsley and egg. Serve with crackers. Makes about 3 cups.

TIP For quick microwave oven clean-up, heat about ½ cup water to boiling in the oven. The steam will help any cooked-on food come off more easily.

Chicken-Stuffed Mushrooms

1 package (16 ounces) Campbell's Fresh Mushrooms
2 tablespoons finely chopped celery
2 tablespoons finely chopped onion
1 tablespoon butter or margarine
½ cup soft bread crumbs
½ cup shredded Monterey Jack cheese (2 ounces)
Generous dash salt
Generous dash pepper
1 can (5 ounces) Swanson Premium Chunk White Chicken, drained

1. Remove mushroom stems. Chop enough stems to measure ½ cup; reserve remaining stems for another use.

2. Arrange mushroom caps, stem-side down, on 10-inch microwave-safe plate lined with paper towels, placing large caps around outside. Microwave, uncovered, on HIGH 2 minutes or until most mushrooms are tender.

3. In 1-quart microwave-safe bowl, combine the ½ cup mushroom stems, celery, onion and butter. Cover with vented plastic wrap; microwave on HIGH 3 minutes or until vegetables are tender, stirring once during cooking.

4. Stir in crumbs, cheese, salt and pepper. Add chicken; toss gently to mix.

5. Spoon chicken mixture into mushroom caps. Arrange stuffed caps on same 10-inch plate lined with clean paper towels, placing less-tender mushrooms around outside. Microwave, uncovered, on HIGH 2½ minutes or until mushrooms are tender. Makes about 20 appetizers.

Spicy Warmer

2 cups "V8" Vegetable Juice
1 teaspoon Worcestershire sauce
½ teaspoon prepared horseradish
¼ teaspoon hot pepper sauce

In 4-cup glass measure, stir together all ingredients. Cover with vented plastic wrap; microwave on HIGH 3 minutes or until boiling. Makes about 2 cups or 3 servings.

Pickled Pepper Quiche

¼ **pound bulk pork sausage**
4 **eggs**
1 **can (10¾ ounces) Campbell's Condensed Cream of**
    Chicken Soup
½ **cup half-and-half or milk**
¼ **cup chopped Vlasic Mild Pepper Rings**
2 **tablespoons chopped fresh parsley**
¼ **teaspoon paprika**
1 **(9-inch) piecrust, baked in microwave-safe pie plate**

1. Crumble sausage into small microwave-safe bowl. Cover with paper towel; microwave on HIGH 5 minutes or until pork is no longer pink, stirring once during cooking to break up meat. Drain on paper towels; set aside.

2. In large bowl, beat eggs and soup until smooth. Stir in half-and-half, chopped pepper rings, parsley, paprika and sausage. Pour into piecrust.

3. Elevate if necessary (see page 7). Microwave, uncovered, at 50% power 22 minutes or until center is nearly set, rotating dish 3 times during cooking. Let stand directly on countertop 10 minutes. Garnish with additional pepper rings. Makes 12 appetizer servings.

Fireside Cup

3 **cups "V8" Vegetable Juice**
1 **cup apple juice**
1 **cinnamon stick**
3 **whole cloves**

In 4-cup glass measure, stir together all ingredients. Cover with vented plastic wrap; microwave on HIGH 5 minutes or until very hot. Remove cinnamon stick and cloves before serving. Makes about 4 cups or 4 servings.

PICKLED PEPPER QUICHE ▶

Southwestern Zucchini Quiche

*Feature this crustless quiche as a brunch entrée along with mixed
fruit and corn bread.*

   1 tablespoon butter or margarine
   1 cup chopped zucchini
   1 cup chopped Campbell's Fresh Mushrooms
   1/2 cup chopped onion
   1/4 cup chopped sweet red pepper
   1 clove garlic, minced
   1/4 teaspoon dried basil leaves, crushed
   1/4 teaspoon dried oregano leaves, crushed
   1 can (11 ounces) Campbell's Condensed Nacho Cheese
      Soup/Dip
   3 eggs, beaten
   2 cups shredded Monterey Jack cheese (8 ounces)
   1 tablespoon all-purpose flour

1. Place butter in 10-inch microwave-safe pie plate. Cover; microwave on
HIGH 20 seconds or until butter melts. Brush butter over bottom and side of
pie plate; set aside.

2. In 2-quart microwave-safe casserole, combine zucchini, mushrooms,
onion, red pepper, garlic, basil and oregano. Cover with lid; microwave on
HIGH 4 minutes or until vegetables are tender, stirring once during cooking.

3. Stir in soup; stir in eggs, cheese and flour until well blended. Pour into
prepared pie plate.

4. Elevate if necessary (see page 7). Microwave, uncovered, on HIGH 13
minutes or until center is nearly set, rotating dish 3 times during cooking. Let
stand directly on countertop 10 minutes. Makes 12 appetizer servings or 4
main dish servings.

Mushroom and Leek Tart

1 tablespoon butter or margarine
2 cups finely chopped leeks
1½ cups sliced Campbell's Fresh Mushrooms
1 can (10¾ ounces) Campbell's Condensed Cream of
    Celery Soup
4 eggs, beaten
1 cup shredded Swiss cheese (4 ounces)
½ cup half-and-half or milk
1 tablespoon all-purpose flour
⅛ teaspoon ground red pepper (cayenne)
⅛ teaspoon ground nutmeg

1. In 2-quart microwave-safe casserole, combine butter, leeks and mushrooms. Cover with lid; microwave on HIGH 6 minutes or until vegetables are tender, stirring once during cooking. Spoon off any excess liquid.

2. In medium bowl, stir soup until smooth; stir in eggs, cheese, half-and-half, flour, pepper and nutmeg. Stir in leek mixture until well blended. Pour into 9-inch microwave-safe pie plate.

3. Elevate if necessary (see page 7). Microwave, uncovered, at 50% power 22 minutes or until center is nearly set, rotating dish 3 times during cooking. Let stand directly on countertop 10 minutes. Makes 8 appetizer servings.

Note: Be sure to remove grit from leeks before chopping. To clean leeks, simply cut them in half lengthwise and rinse away sand with running water.

TIP At 50% power your microwave oven will cycle on and off. The length of this cycle varies from oven to oven and can be as much as one minute in length (30 seconds on and 30 seconds off). When you use a reduced power level for less than one minute, the results may be hard to predict because you may not be sure where you entered the cycle. Instead of using a low power level for such a short time, microwave the food on HIGH, checking frequently, or place a cup of water alongside the food to absorb some of the microwave energy.

White Pita Pizzas

The creamy onion sauce on these pizzas is a wonderful base for imaginative toppings. We've suggested two, but add your own favorite traditional and non-traditional garnishes. Some ideas for toppings are pepperoni, anchovies, capers, yellow peppers, and fresh basil leaves.

1 can (10¾ ounces) Campbell's Condensed Creamy Onion Soup/Dip
2 tablespoons milk
2 tablespoons chopped fresh parsley
1 clove garlic, minced
6 pita bread rounds (6-inch), split horizontally and toasted
⅓ cup roasted red pepper cut into strips
⅓ cup sliced pitted ripe olives
1 cup shredded mozzarella cheese (4 ounces)

1. In 1-quart microwave-safe casserole, stir soup until smooth. Stir in milk, parsley and garlic until well blended. Cover with lid; microwave on HIGH 3 minutes or until very hot, stirring once during cooking.

2. Spread heaping tablespoonful of soup mixture over each pita half. Top with some of the pepper strips, olives and cheese.

3. Arrange 4 pita halves on 10-inch microwave-safe plate lined with paper towel. Microwave, uncovered, on HIGH 1½ minutes or until cheese is melted. Repeat twice with remaining pizzas. Makes 12 appetizer servings.

Note: If you don't need this quantity all at once, simply store toasted pita halves in an airtight bag at room temperature and refrigerate toppings and soup mixture, covered, up to 3 days. You can assemble and microwave a plate of pizzas in minutes.

TIP   Although you keep cheese in the refrigerator, it tastes better at room temperature. To bring it to eating temperature, wrap 2 ounces or more in waxed paper and microwave on HIGH, checking every 10 to 15 seconds.

Sunny Sipper

1½ cups "V8" Vegetable Juice
½ cup orange juice
1 tablespoon lemon or lime juice
1 tablespoon honey

In 4-cup glass measure, stir together all ingredients. Cover with vented plastic wrap; microwave on HIGH 3 minutes or until boiling. Makes about 2 cups or 2 servings.

> **TIP**   Hot chocolate couldn't be easier to prepare. Pour chocolate milk into a microwave-safe mug and heat in the microwave oven. Other great beverages to heat right in a mug include apple cider, "V8" Vegetable Juice, beef broth and chicken broth. Sake (Japanese rice wine) can be warmed in a microwave-safe serving carafe or in individual cups.

Mini Reubens

Your microwave oven helps you heat appetizers in minutes. Toast the bread early in the day, then assemble the Mini Reubens just before heating.

20 slices Pepperidge Farm Party Rye or Pumpernickel
Bread, toasted
¼ pound thinly sliced cooked corned beef
¼ cup Thousand Island dressing
1 cup Vlasic Sauerkraut, rinsed and drained
1 cup shredded Swiss cheese (4 ounces)

1. Arrange bread on 2 large microwave-safe plates lined with paper towels. Top each bread slice with small piece of corned beef, some dressing, sauerkraut and Swiss cheese.

2. Microwave 1 plate at a time, uncovered, on HIGH 1 minute or until cheese is melted. Makes 20 appetizers.

Note: Full-size slices of rye or pumpernickel bread can be used in place of the party rye. Cut bread into festive shapes with a cookie cutter. Toast cutouts, then assemble sandwiches as directed.

Soups

Golden Broccoli Soup

 2 cups broccoli flowerets
½ cup shredded carrot
½ cup chopped onion
¼ cup water
 1 can (10¾ ounces) Campbell's Condensed Creamy
    Natural Potato Soup
 1 soup can milk
 1 cup shredded Cheddar cheese (4 ounces)
¼ teaspoon pepper

1. In 3-quart microwave-safe casserole, combine broccoli, carrot, onion and water. Cover with lid; microwave on HIGH 5 minutes or until vegetables are tender.

2. In small bowl, stir soup until smooth. Stir in milk, cheese and pepper; mix well. Stir into vegetables. Cover; microwave on HIGH 8 minutes or until hot and bubbling, stirring twice during cooking. Let stand, covered, 5 minutes. Makes 4 cups or 4 servings.

GOLDEN BROCCOLI SOUP ▶

Cucumber-Leek Soup

**2 cans (10¾ ounces each) Campbell's Condensed
    Chicken Broth**
½ cup water
1 large cucumber, peeled, seeded and sliced
1 large leek, sliced (white part only)
2 tablespoons chopped fresh parsley
**1 teaspoon fresh dill weed or ½ teaspoon dried dill
    weed, crushed**
⅛ teaspoon pepper
¼ cup plain yogurt

1. In 2-quart microwave-safe casserole, combine broth, water, cucumber and leek. Cover with lid; microwave on HIGH 8 minutes or until boiling.

2. With slotted spoon, remove vegetables to blender or food processor. Add ½ cup of the broth mixture, parsley, dill and pepper. Cover; blend until smooth. Return mixture to broth. Cover; microwave on HIGH 4 minutes or until hot and bubbling.

3. Ladle soup into bowls; top with yogurt and garnish with additional dill weed. Makes about 4 cups or 4 servings.

TIP In high-altitude areas, food will microwave more slowly, although it may boil vigorously. For liquid mixtures such as soups, you may need a larger container; also remove the cover if it's boiling too hard. Sometimes increasing the power by one level may help compensate for lower boiling temperatures; otherwise add more time. Liquids tend to evaporate more quickly at high altitudes, so you may need to add more water or liquid.

Hearty Borscht

2 tablespoons butter or margarine
½ cup chopped onion
**1 can (16 ounces) whole beets, drained and coarsely
   chopped**
2 cups coarsely chopped cabbage
**1 can (10¾ ounces) Campbell's Home Cookin' Old
   Fashioned Vegetable Beef Soup**
**1 can (10½ ounces) Campbell's Condensed Beef Broth
   (Bouillon)**
1 cup water
1 tablespoon lemon juice
1 teaspoon sugar
¼ teaspoon pepper
½ cup sour cream for garnish
**2 tablespoons chopped chives or green onions for
   garnish**

1. In 3-quart microwave-safe casserole, combine butter and onion. Cover
with lid; microwave on HIGH 3 minutes or until tender, stirring once during
cooking.

2. Stir in beets, cabbage, soup, broth, water, lemon juice, sugar and pepper.
Cover; microwave on HIGH 12 minutes or until boiling, stirring once during
cooking. Let stand, covered, 5 minutes.

3. Meanwhile, in small bowl, stir together sour cream and chives. Ladle soup
into bowls and garnish with sour cream mixture. Makes about 6½ cups or
4 servings.

Curried Zucchini Soup

For an elegant presentation, serve bowls of chilled soup in liners packed with crushed ice.

1 tablespoon butter or margarine
2 cups coarsely chopped zucchini
2 tablespoons sliced green onion
1 teaspoon curry powder
1 can (10¾ ounces) Campbell's Condensed Cream of
    Potato Soup
1¾ cups milk
    Pepperidge Farm Croutons for garnish

1. In 2-quart microwave-safe casserole, combine butter, zucchini, onion and curry powder. Cover with lid; microwave on HIGH 7 minutes or until zucchini is very tender, stirring once during cooking.

2. Stir soup into zucchini mixture. In covered blender or food processor, blend soup mixture until smooth. Return to casserole. Stir in milk.

3. Cover; refrigerate until serving time, at least 4 hours. Thin chilled soup to desired consistency with additional milk. Ladle into bowls and garnish with croutons. Makes about 4 cups or 4 servings.

Note: To serve this soup hot, prepare as above through step 2. Cover; microwave on HIGH 4 minutes or until hot and bubbling.

Fresh Spinach Soup

1 tablespoon butter or margarine
2 cups loosely packed chopped spinach leaves
1 can (10¾ ounces) Campbell's Condensed Cream of
    Potato Soup
1 soup can milk
2 tablespoons dry sherry or vermouth
    Dash ground nutmeg

1. In 2-quart microwave-safe casserole, combine butter and spinach. Cover with lid; microwave on HIGH 2 minutes or until spinach is wilted.

2. Stir in soup until smooth; stir in milk, sherry and nutmeg until well blended. Cover; microwave on HIGH 6 minutes or until hot and bubbling, stirring once during cooking. Makes about 3 cups or 4 servings.

CURRIED ZUCCHINI SOUP ▶

Apple-Cheese Soup

This soup is equally delicious served hot or cold.

2 apples, peeled and chopped
1 tablespoon water
¼ teaspoon ground nutmeg
¼ teaspoon ground cinnamon
**1 can (11 ounces) Campbell's Condensed Cheddar
    Cheese Soup/Sauce**
¾ cup milk
Sour cream or plain yogurt for garnish

1. In 2-quart microwave-safe casserole, combine apples, water, nutmeg and cinnamon. Cover with lid; microwave on HIGH 5 minutes or until apples are very tender, stirring once during cooking.

2. Stir soup into apple mixture. In covered blender or food processor, blend soup mixture until smooth. Return to casserole. Stir in milk. Cover; microwave on HIGH 3 minutes or until hot and bubbling. Garnish with sour cream and additional nutmeg. Makes about 3 cups or 4 servings.

California Bisque

1 tablespoon butter or margarine
¼ cup thinly sliced celery
½ teaspoon chili powder
Generous dash ground cinnamon
**1 can (11 ounces) Campbell's Condensed Tomato Bisque
    Soup**
1 soup can water
2 teaspoons lemon juice
½ cup chopped avocado

1. In 1½-quart microwave-safe casserole, combine butter, celery, chili powder and cinnamon. Cover with lid; microwave on HIGH 3 minutes or until celery is tender, stirring once during cooking.

2. Stir in soup, water and lemon juice. Cover; microwave on HIGH 3 minutes or until hot and bubbling. Stir in avocado. Makes about 3 cups or 3 servings.

Chilled Cream of Parsley Soup

1 tablespoon butter or margarine
1½ cups finely chopped fresh parsley
1 can (10¾ ounces) Campbell's Condensed Cream of
    Celery Soup
1 soup can milk
1 egg yolk
1 tablespoon lemon juice
    Dash ground red pepper (cayenne)
½ cup heavy cream, whipped

1. In 2-quart microwave-safe casserole, combine butter and parsley. Cover with lid; microwave on HIGH 3 minutes or until parsley is wilted.

2. Stir in soup until smooth; stir in milk. Cover; microwave on HIGH 7 minutes or until boiling.

3. In small bowl, beat egg yolk. Slowly beat ½ cup hot soup into yolk. Return egg mixture to soup. Stir in lemon juice and pepper. Carefully pour into blender or food processor. Cover; blend until smooth.

4. Return to casserole. Cover; refrigerate until serving time, at least 4 hours. Garnish with whipped cream and additional parsley leaves. Makes about 3 cups or 4 servings.

TIP   Your microwave oven makes it easy to cook faster, but how can you *cool* foods faster? One way is to put the warm food into a bowl, then set that into a larger bowl of ice and water. If the hot food can be stirred without hurting it (such as a soup or stew), constant stirring will help cool the food even faster. Don't stir foods that might break up and become unattractive (potato salad, for example).

Oriental Vegetable Soup

2 cans (14½ ounces each) Swanson Clear Ready to Serve
    Chicken Broth
1 tablespoon soy sauce
1 tablespoon dry sherry
⅛ teaspoon grated fresh ginger
½ cup fresh or frozen cut green beans
¼ cup thinly sliced carrot
¼ cup cubed tofu

1. In 2-quart microwave-safe casserole, stir together broth, soy sauce, sherry and ginger. Stir in beans and carrot. Cover with lid; microwave on HIGH 10 minutes or until soup is boiling and vegetables are tender-crisp.

2. Stir in tofu. Let stand, covered, 2 minutes. Makes about 5 cups or 6 servings.

Note: To make carrot flowers: Use an hors d'oeuvre cutter or sharp knife to cut carrot slices into flower shapes. For easier cutting, microwave whole carrot on HIGH 1 minute or until slightly softened.

Egg Drop Soup

2 cans (14½ ounces each) Swanson Clear Ready to Serve
    Chicken Broth
1 tablespoon cornstarch
1 tablespoon rice wine vinegar or dry sherry
2 teaspoons soy sauce
½ cup cooked ham cut into thin strips
½ cup snow peas
3 green onions, sliced
2 eggs, beaten

1. In 2-quart microwave-safe casserole, stir together broth, cornstarch, vinegar and soy sauce until smooth; stir in ham, snow peas and onions. Cover with lid; microwave on HIGH 10 minutes or until boiling, stirring twice during cooking.

2. With fork, stir broth in swirling motion. Without stirring, slowly pour eggs into swirling broth; then stir just until eggs are set in long strands. Makes about 4 cups or 4 servings.

ORIENTAL VEGETABLE SOUP ▶

Greek Lemon Soup

Orzo is a small rice-shaped pasta that is traditional in this classic Greek soup.

2 cans (14½ ounces each) Swanson Clear Ready to Serve Chicken Broth
¼ cup orzo or regular long-grain rice, uncooked
2 eggs
2 tablespoons lemon juice
Thin lemon slices for garnish

1. In 2-quart microwave-safe casserole, combine broth and orzo. Cover with lid; microwave on HIGH 8 minutes or until boiling. Stir soup.

2. Reduce power to 50%. Cover; microwave 18 minutes or until orzo is tender, stirring once during cooking.

3. In small bowl, beat eggs with lemon juice. Slowly beat ½ cup hot soup into egg mixture. Return egg mixture to broth, stirring constantly until soup is slightly thickened. Garnish with lemon slices. Makes about 4 cups or 4 servings.

TIP Freeze small amounts of leftover chicken broth, pesto or tomato sauce in ice cube trays. When frozen, store cubes in a freezer bag until ready to use. Microwave 1 or 2 cubes in a custard cup until melted.

Double Onion Soup Gratinée

Easier to eat and easier to use than traditional French bread slices, croutons also add more flavor to this updated soup.

1 tablespoon butter or margarine
2 green onions, thinly sliced
1 can (10½ ounces) Campbell's Condensed French Onion Soup
1 soup can water
2 tablespoons dry vermouth
1 cup Pepperidge Farm Onion and Garlic Croutons
1 cup shredded Swiss cheese (4 ounces)

1. In 4-cup glass measure, combine butter and onions. Microwave, uncovered, on HIGH 1 minute or until onions are wilted.

2. Stir in soup, water and vermouth. Microwave, uncovered, on HIGH 5 minutes or until boiling, stirring once during cooking.

3. Ladle soup into four 10-ounce bowls. Sprinkle croutons over soup; sprinkle with cheese. Let stand, uncovered, 1 minute or until cheese is melted. Makes about 3 cups or 4 servings.

Southern Tomato-Bean Soup

Serve this hearty soup with corn bread for added Southern flavor.

1 tablespoon vegetable oil or bacon drippings
½ cup chopped celery
½ cup chopped onion
1 clove garlic, minced
¼ teaspoon dried thyme leaves, crushed
1 can (16 ounces) Campbell's Pork & Beans in Tomato Sauce
1 can (14½ ounces) tomatoes, undrained, cut up
⅛ teaspoon black pepper
⅛ teaspoon ground red pepper (cayenne)

1. In 2-quart microwave-safe casserole, combine oil, celery, onion, garlic and thyme. Cover with lid; microwave on HIGH 3 minutes or until vegetables are tender, stirring once during cooking.

2. Stir in pork and beans, tomatoes with their liquid, black pepper and red pepper. Cover; microwave on HIGH 8 minutes or until hot and bubbling, stirring once during cooking. Makes about 4 cups or 4 servings.

Bavarian Pea Soup

1 tablespoon butter or margarine
1/2 cup shredded cabbage
1/4 teaspoon caraway seeds
1 can (19 ounces) Campbell's Home Cookin' Split Pea
    with Ham or Chunky Split Pea 'n Ham Soup
Pumpernickel bread, torn into pieces
Shredded Swiss cheese

1. In 1-quart microwave-safe casserole, combine butter, cabbage and caraway. Cover with lid; microwave on HIGH 3 minutes or until cabbage is tender, stirring once during cooking.

2. Stir in soup. Cover; microwave on HIGH 4 minutes or until heated through, stirring once during cooking.

3. Pour soup into 2 microwave-safe soup bowls; top with bread and cheese. Microwave, uncovered, on HIGH 1 minute or until cheese is melted. Makes 2 servings.

Lettuce and Chicken Soup

2 1/2 cups water
1 pouch Campbell's Chicken Noodle Soup and Recipe
    Mix
1/2 cup shredded carrot
1/4 cup sliced green onions
2 teaspoons lemon juice
1 cup shredded lettuce

1. Pour water into 2-quart microwave-safe casserole. Cover with lid; microwave on HIGH 6 minutes or until boiling.

2. Stir in soup mix, carrot, green onions and lemon juice. Microwave, uncovered, on HIGH 4 minutes or until chicken is tender. Stir in lettuce. Let stand, covered, 5 minutes. Makes about 3 cups or 3 servings.

BAVARIAN PEA SOUP ▶

Creamy Fish Chowder

4 slices bacon, chopped
1 cup thinly sliced carrots
½ cup chopped onion
1 can (10¾ ounces) Campbell's Condensed Cream of
    Potato Soup
1½ cups milk
  ½ pound firm white fish, cut into chunks
2 tablespoons chopped fresh parsley

1. Place bacon in 2-quart microwave-safe casserole. Cover with paper towel; microwave on HIGH 3 minutes or until crisp, stirring once during cooking. Remove bacon to paper towels, reserving drippings in casserole.

2. Add carrots and onion to drippings. Cover with lid; microwave on HIGH 4 minutes or until vegetables are tender, stirring once during cooking.

3. Stir in soup, milk, fish and parsley until well mixed. Cover; microwave on HIGH 9 minutes or until fish flakes easily with fork, stirring once during cooking. Garnish with reserved bacon. Makes about 4 cups or 4 servings.

Tuna Chowder: Substitute 1 can (6½ ounces) tuna, drained and flaked, for white fish. In step 3, microwave on HIGH only 4 minutes or until bubbling.

Note: To substitute Mrs. Paul's Frozen Au Naturel Cod Fillets for white fish: Separate fillets from 1 package (10 ounces) Mrs. Paul's Frozen Au Naturel Cod Fillets. Arrange on microwave-safe plate. Microwave, uncovered, on HIGH 1 minute or until fish is pliable; cut into chunks. Proceed as above, stirring contents of seasoning packet into chowder along with fish.

TIP　Don't forget disposable containers. Heatsafe paper cups and bowls are great for melting butter or chocolate, or for cooking small quantities of foods such as a single serving of soup or a scrambled egg. Best of all, when you're through, there's nothing to wash!

Chicken-Corn Soup Santa Fe

1 tablespoon butter or margarine
1 clove garlic, minced
1 can (10¾ ounces) Campbell's Condensed Chicken
    Broth
1 soup can water
1 can (8 ounces) cream-style golden corn
1 can (5 ounces) Swanson Premium Chunk White
    Chicken, undrained
½ teaspoon finely chopped Vlasic Jalapeño Peppers
¼ teaspoon ground cumin
    Tortilla chips

1. In 2-quart microwave-safe casserole, combine butter and garlic. Cover with lid; microwave on HIGH 30 seconds or until butter is melted.

2. Stir in broth, water, corn, chicken, peppers and cumin. Cover; microwave on HIGH 5 minutes or until hot and bubbling. Place a few tortilla chips in each of four 10-ounce soup bowls. Ladle hot soup over chips. Makes about 4 cups or 4 servings.

Lentil-Pasta Soup

1 tablespoon olive or vegetable oil
1 cup chopped onion
2 cloves garlic, minced
1 can (19 ounces) Campbell's Home Cookin' Lentil Soup
1 can (14½ ounces) Swanson Clear Ready to Serve Beef
    Broth
½ cup chopped fresh parsley
½ teaspoon dried basil leaves, crushed
½ teaspoon dried oregano leaves, crushed
½ cup small shell pasta, uncooked

1. In 3-quart microwave-safe casserole, combine oil, onion and garlic. Cover with lid; microwave on HIGH 3 minutes or until onion is tender, stirring once during cooking.

2. Stir in soup and broth. Cover; microwave on HIGH 8 minutes or until very hot. Stir in parsley, basil, oregano and pasta. Cover; microwave on HIGH 13 minutes or until pasta is tender, stirring twice during cooking. Let stand, covered, 5 minutes. Makes about 4 cups or 3 servings.

Poultry

Country Captain

2½ pounds chicken parts, skinned
1 can (11 ounces) Campbell's Condensed Zesty Tomato Soup/Sauce
1 green pepper, cut into ½-inch pieces
¼ cup raisins
1 teaspoon curry powder
¼ cup toasted slivered almonds (see Note on page 125)
Hot cooked rice

1. Arrange chicken in 12- by 8-inch microwave-safe baking dish, placing thicker portions toward edges of dish.

2. In small bowl, stir together soup, green pepper, raisins and curry powder. Spoon soup mixture over chicken.

3. Cover with waxed paper; microwave on HIGH 22 minutes or until chicken is nearly done, rearranging chicken and basting with pan juices once during cooking. Let stand, covered, 5 minutes or until chicken is no longer pink in center. Sprinkle with almonds; serve over rice. Makes 6 servings.

COUNTRY CAPTAIN ▶

Italian Chicken

2½ pounds chicken parts, skinned
1 cup sliced Campbell's Fresh Mushrooms
½ cup chopped onion
1 jar (15½ ounces) Prego Spaghetti Sauce

1. Arrange chicken in 12- by 8-inch microwave-safe baking dish, placing thicker portions toward edges of dish. Top with mushrooms and onion. Pour spaghetti sauce over chicken.

2. Cover with waxed paper; microwave on HIGH 22 minutes or until chicken is nearly done, rearranging chicken parts once during cooking. Let stand, covered, 5 minutes or until chicken is no longer pink in center. Makes 6 servings.

Arroz con Pollo

1 tablespoon olive or vegetable oil
1 clove garlic, minced
1 can (10¾ ounces) Campbell's Condensed Chicken Broth
1 can (8 ounces) tomatoes, undrained, cut up
¾ cup regular long-grain rice, uncooked
⅛ teaspoon ground turmeric
2 pounds chicken thighs, skinned
1 cup frozen peas

1. In 12- by 8-inch microwave-safe baking dish, combine oil and garlic. Cover with vented plastic wrap; microwave on HIGH 1 minute.

2. Stir in broth and tomatoes with their liquid. Cover; microwave on HIGH 5 minutes or until boiling.

3. Stir in rice and turmeric. Arrange chicken thighs over rice, with thicker portions toward edges of dish. Cover; microwave on HIGH 8 minutes.

4. Remove chicken. Stir peas into rice; rearrange chicken over rice. Cover; microwave on HIGH 15 minutes or until rice is nearly done, rotating dish once during cooking. Let stand, covered, 10 minutes or until rice is tender and chicken is no longer pink in center. Makes 6 servings.

Glorified Chicken

2¹/₂ pounds chicken parts, skinned
1 can (10³/₄ ounces) Campbell's Condensed Cream of Chicken, Cream of Mushroom or Golden Mushroom Soup
2 tablespoons chopped fresh parsley

1. Arrange chicken in 12- by 8-inch microwave-safe baking dish, placing thicker portions toward edges of dish.

2. In small bowl, stir soup until smooth; stir in parsley. Spread soup evenly over chicken.

3. Cover with waxed paper; microwave on HIGH 20 minutes or until chicken is nearly done, rearranging chicken and basting with pan juices once during cooking. Let stand, covered, 5 minutes or until chicken is no longer pink in center. Makes 6 servings.

Chicken with Sweet Potatoes

2 tablespoons butter or margarine
1 pound sweet potatoes, peeled and cubed (3 cups)
1 can (10³/₄ ounces) Campbell's Condensed Cream of Chicken Soup
2 tablespoons dry sherry
1 tablespoon orange juice
¹/₄ teaspoon rubbed sage
4 skinless boneless chicken breast halves (about 1 pound)
Orange slices for garnish

1. In 3-quart microwave-safe casserole, combine butter and sweet potatoes. Cover with lid; microwave on HIGH 5 minutes or until potatoes are nearly tender, stirring once during cooking.

2. In small bowl, stir soup until smooth; stir in sherry, orange juice and sage.

3. Arrange chicken in circular pattern over sweet potatoes. Pour soup mixture over chicken. Cover; microwave on HIGH 15 minutes or until chicken is nearly done, rotating dish once during cooking. Let stand, covered, 5 minutes or until chicken is no longer pink in center. Garnish with orange slices. Makes 4 servings.

Rolled Chicken Breasts Florentine

**4 skinless boneless chicken breast halves (about
1 pound)**
4 thin slices (1 ounce each) cooked ham
4 thin slices (1 ounce each) Swiss cheese
**1 package (10 ounces) frozen chopped spinach, thawed
and well drained**
**1 can (10¾ ounces) Campbell's Condensed Golden
Mushroom or Cream of Chicken Soup**
⅓ cup water
¼ cup sliced green onions
⅛ teaspoon dried thyme leaves, crushed

1. With flat side of meat mallet, pound chicken to ¼-inch thickness. Place a ham slice, cheese slice and ¼ of the spinach on each chicken piece. Roll up chicken from short end, jelly-roll fashion. Secure with wooden toothpicks if needed.

2. Place chicken, seam-side down, in 12- by 8-inch microwave-safe baking dish. Cover with vented plastic wrap; microwave on HIGH 5 minutes.

3. In small bowl, stir soup until smooth; stir in water, onions and thyme. Pour over chicken. Cover; microwave on HIGH 10 minutes or until chicken is nearly done, rotating dish once during cooking. Let stand, covered, 5 minutes or until chicken is fork-tender. Makes 4 servings.

Note: To thaw 1 package (10 ounces) frozen spinach: Place frozen spinach in 1½-quart microwave-safe casserole. Cover with lid; microwave on HIGH 5 minutes, stirring once during heating. Drain thoroughly.

TIP   Most of our chicken recipes suggest that you remove the chicken skin before cooking. Microwave-cooked chicken skin is usually unattractive because it doesn't brown or crisp. Removing it gives you a bonus of fewer calories, too.

Chicken in Wine Sauce

4 slices bacon, chopped
1 cup carrots cut into matchstick-thin strips
1 pouch Campbell's Onion Mushroom Soup and Recipe
    Mix
1 cup water
1/2 cup Chablis or other dry white wine
1/8 teaspoon pepper
 4 skinless boneless chicken breast halves (about
      1 pound)

1. Place bacon in 3-quart microwave-safe casserole. Cover with paper towel; microwave on HIGH 3 minutes or until crisp, stirring once during cooking. Remove bacon to paper towels, reserving drippings in casserole.

2. Add carrots to drippings. Cover with lid; microwave on HIGH 3 minutes or until carrots are tender. Stir in soup mix, water, wine and pepper until well blended.

3. Add chicken breasts, placing thicker portions toward edge of dish. Cover; microwave on HIGH 10 minutes or until chicken is nearly done, rearranging chicken once during cooking. Let stand, covered, 5 minutes or until chicken is no longer pink in center. Sprinkle with reserved bacon. Makes 4 servings.

TIP   If you're going to use your microwave oven to cook more than one dish for a meal, follow these guidelines.
• Cook only one dish at a time. If two are cooked together, they will interfere with the microwave absorption of each other.
• The first dish cooked should be the one with the longer cooking time and the one that can retain its heat longer. Generally, denser foods, such as casseroles, stews or meats, hold their heat better.
• If one food cools off before serving, reheat it briefly.
• If a dessert can be served warm, cook it during the meal.

Mushroom-Stuffed Chicken Breasts

Stuffing mix makes a deliciously crisp coating for this chicken.
Crush it with a rolling pin or in a blender or food processor.

4 tablespoons butter or margarine
1½ cups chopped Campbell's Fresh Mushrooms
¼ cup chopped green onions
¼ cup finely chopped celery
¼ teaspoon dried marjoram leaves, crushed
2 cups Pepperidge Farm Herb Seasoned Stuffing Mix,
    coarsely crushed
4 skinless boneless chicken breast halves (about
    1 pound)
1 egg
2 tablespoons milk
1 teaspoon paprika

1. In 2-quart microwave-safe casserole, combine 2 tablespoons of the butter, mushrooms, onions, celery and marjoram. Cover with lid; microwave on HIGH 4 minutes or until vegetables are tender, stirring once during cooking. Stir in ½ cup of the stuffing mix until blended; set aside.

2. With flat side of meat mallet, pound chicken to ¼-inch thickness. Divide stuffing among breast halves. Roll up chicken from short end, jelly-roll fashion. Secure with wooden toothpicks if needed.

3. In small bowl, beat egg and milk. In pie plate, combine remaining 1½ cups stuffing mix and paprika. Dip rolled breasts in egg mixture, then in stuffing mixture. Place chicken, seam-side down, in 12- by 8-inch microwave-safe baking dish.

4. Place remaining 2 tablespoons butter in small microwave-safe bowl. Microwave on HIGH 30 seconds or until melted. Drizzle over chicken.

5. Cover with waxed paper; microwave on HIGH 8 minutes or until chicken is nearly done, rotating dish once during cooking. Let stand, covered, 5 minutes or until chicken is no longer pink in center. Makes 4 servings.

Note: For even crisper chicken, prepare as directed above. Transfer chicken to broiler pan; broil 4 inches from heat 1 to 2 minutes or until top is browned.

Chicken and Mushroom Kabobs

¼ cup soy sauce
¼ cup packed brown sugar
2 tablespoons dry sherry
1 tablespoon grated fresh ginger
1 tablespoon vegetable oil
1 pound skinless boneless chicken breasts, cut into
    1-inch pieces
1 package (12 ounces) Campbell's Fresh Mushrooms
1 green pepper, cut into 1-inch pieces

1. In large bowl, stir together soy sauce, sugar, sherry, ginger and oil. Stir in chicken and mushrooms. Cover; marinate in refrigerator 1 hour.

2. On eight 10-inch wooden skewers, alternately thread chicken, mushrooms and green pepper, leaving small spaces between pieces. Arrange skewers across 12- by 8-inch microwave-safe baking dish. Microwave, uncovered, on HIGH 12 minutes or until chicken is no longer pink in center, rearranging kabobs and basting with marinade twice during cooking. Makes 4 servings.

Turkey Meatballs

1 pound ground turkey
1 egg
½ cup fine dry bread crumbs
¼ cup finely chopped onion
1 can (10½ ounces) Franco-American Turkey Gravy
⅓ cup apple jelly
⅓ cup chili sauce
    Hot cooked thin noodles

1. In large bowl, thoroughly blend turkey, egg, crumbs, onion and ¼ cup of the gravy. Shape into 1-inch meatballs; set aside.

2. In 3-quart microwave-safe casserole, stir together remaining gravy, jelly and chili sauce. Cover with waxed paper; microwave on HIGH 5 minutes or until jelly is melted, stirring once during cooking.

3. Add meatballs to gravy mixture. Cover; microwave on HIGH 8 minutes or until meatballs are no longer pink, stirring once during cooking. Let stand, covered, 5 minutes. Serve over noodles. Makes 4 servings.

Turkey and Stuffing Casserole

1/4 cup butter or margarine, cut up
  1 package (7 ounces) Pepperidge Farm Herb Seasoned
    Cube Stuffing Mix
  1 can (10¾ ounces) Campbell's Condensed Cream of
    Chicken Soup
1/2 cup milk
  2 cups cubed cooked turkey or chicken (about
    12 ounces)
  1 cup coarsely chopped celery
  1 package (10 ounces) frozen chopped broccoli, cooked
    and drained
3/4 cup shredded Cheddar cheese (3 ounces)

1. Place butter in large microwave-safe bowl. Cover; microwave on HIGH 40 seconds or until melted. Add stuffing mix; toss to coat evenly. Set aside.

2. In large bowl, stir soup until smooth. Stir in milk; stir in turkey, celery and broccoli.

3. Spread ½ of the stuffing mixture in 12- by 8-inch microwave-safe baking dish. Spread soup mixture over stuffing. Cover with waxed paper; microwave on HIGH 10 minutes or until heated through, rotating dish once during cooking.

4. Top with remaining stuffing mixture; sprinkle with cheese. Microwave, uncovered, on HIGH 1 minute. Let stand, uncovered, 5 minutes. Makes 4 servings.

Glazed Stuffed Cornish Hens

2 Cornish hens (1½ pounds each)
¼ cup butter or margarine
½ cup chopped onion
½ cup sweet red pepper cut into matchstick-thin strips
½ cup green pepper cut into matchstick-thin strips
1 package (8 ounces) Pepperidge Farm Herb Seasoned Stuffing Mix
1 cup Swanson Clear Ready to Serve Chicken Broth
½ cup apricot preserves

1. Remove giblets and neck from inside hens (reserve for another use if desired). Rinse hens; pat dry. Split hens along backbone and breastbone; set aside.

2. In 3-quart microwave-safe bowl, combine butter, onion and peppers. Cover with vented plastic wrap; microwave on HIGH 3 minutes or until tender, stirring once during cooking. Add stuffing and broth; toss to mix well.

3. Pat stuffing mixture into bottom of 12- by 8-inch microwave-safe baking dish. Arrange hen halves, skin-side up, over stuffing; set aside.

4. Place preserves in small microwave-safe bowl. Microwave, uncovered, on HIGH 45 seconds or until melted. Brush preserves over hens. Cover with waxed paper; microwave on HIGH 17 minutes or until hens are nearly done, rotating dish twice and rearranging hens once during cooking. Let stand, covered, 5 minutes or until hens are no longer pink in center. Makes 4 servings.

TIP   For a special touch after a meal, make warm finger towels. Fold clean, wet washcloths in half, then roll up; place in microwave-safe basket. Microwave on HIGH about 30 seconds. These are also great for cleaning your hands after eating ribs or chicken.

GLAZED STUFFED CORNISH HENS ▶

Springtime Chicken and Rice

1 tablespoon vegetable oil
1/2 cup chopped green pepper
1/2 cup chopped green onions
2 cups cooked rice
1 can (8 ounces) sliced water chestnuts, drained
1/2 cup slivered cooked ham
1 can (5 ounces) Swanson Premium Chunk White
    Chicken, drained
2 eggs

1. In 3-quart microwave-safe casserole, combine oil, green pepper and onions. Cover with lid; microwave on HIGH 4 minutes or until vegetables are tender, stirring once during cooking.

2. Stir in rice, water chestnuts and ham. Cover; microwave on HIGH 5 minutes or until heated through, stirring once during cooking. Stir in chicken. Let stand, covered, 5 minutes.

3. Meanwhile, in small microwave-safe bowl, beat eggs with fork. Cover with vented plastic wrap; microwave on HIGH 1½ minutes or until just set, stirring once during cooking. Cut eggs into thin strips. Stir into rice mixture. Serve with soy sauce, if desired. Makes 5 cups or 4 servings.

Sweet and Sour Chicken

1 teaspoon vegetable oil
2 green onions, cut into 1-inch pieces
1/4 cup sweet red pepper cut into 1/2-inch pieces
1/4 cup green pepper cut into 1/2-inch pieces
1 can (8 ounces) pineapple chunks in juice, undrained
1 tablespoon brown sugar
1 tablespoon rice wine vinegar
2 teaspoons cornstarch
1 can (5 ounces) Swanson Premium Chunk White
    Chicken, drained

1. In 2-quart microwave-safe casserole, combine oil, onions and peppers. Cover with lid; microwave on HIGH 2 minutes or until peppers are nearly tender, stirring once during cooking.

2. Drain pineapple, reserving 3 tablespoons juice. In small bowl, stir together reserved pineapple juice, sugar, vinegar and cornstarch. Stir into vegetable mixture. Stir in pineapple chunks. Cover; microwave on HIGH 3 minutes or until boiling, stirring twice during cooking.

3. Stir in chicken. Cover; microwave on HIGH 2 minutes or until heated through. Serve with cooked rice and soy sauce, if desired. Makes 2 servings.

Chicken and Ham Supreme

1 package (9 ounces) frozen artichoke hearts
1 can (10¾ ounces) Campbell's Condensed Cream of
    Mushroom Soup
½ cup plain yogurt
½ cup shredded Swiss cheese (2 ounces)
1 teaspoon dried basil leaves, crushed
⅛ teaspoon ground red pepper (cayenne)
2 cups cooked rice
1½ cups cubed cooked chicken
1 cup cubed cooked ham
    Chopped fresh parsley for garnish

1. Place artichoke hearts in small microwave-safe bowl. Cover with vented plastic wrap; microwave on HIGH 4 minutes or until heated through, stirring once during cooking. Drain; set aside.

2. In small bowl, stir soup until smooth; stir in yogurt, cheese, basil and pepper.

3. In 8- by 8-inch microwave-safe baking dish, combine rice and ½ cup of the soup mixture; spread evenly in dish. Top with chicken, ham and artichoke hearts. Spoon remaining soup mixture over.

4. Cover with vented plastic wrap; microwave on HIGH 8 minutes or until heated through, rotating dish once during cooking. Let stand, covered, 2 minutes. Garnish with parsley. Makes 4 servings.

Note: Substitute 1 package (about 10 ounces) frozen asparagus or broccoli spears for the artichoke hearts. Cook vegetables according to package directions; drain, then cut into bite-size pieces. Proceed as above in steps 2 through 4.

TIP Even if you never buy a utensil designed for the microwave oven, your shelves probably are full of them: glass measuring cups; glass and ceramic casseroles and mixing bowls; mugs, teacups, bowls and plates made of microwave-safe china; glass and ceramic pie plates and baking dishes.

Creamy Chicken Enchiladas

2 cans (5 ounces each) Swanson Premium Chunk White
    Chicken, drained
½ cup chopped tomato
2 tablespoons chopped green chilies
½ teaspoon dried oregano leaves, crushed
1 can (10¾ ounces) Campbell's Condensed Creamy
    Chicken Mushroom Soup
½ cup sour cream
⅓ cup enchilada sauce
1 tablespoon lemon juice
8 corn tortillas (6-inch)
1 cup shredded Monterey Jack cheese (4 ounces)
    Chopped tomatoes for garnish
    Shredded lettuce for garnish
    Sliced pitted ripe olives for garnish

1. In small bowl, combine chicken, tomato, chilies and oregano; set aside.

2. In 1-quart microwave-safe casserole, stir soup until smooth; stir in sour cream, enchilada sauce and lemon juice. Cover with lid; microwave at 50% power 5 minutes or until heated through, stirring once during cooking. Stir 1 cup of the soup mixture into chicken mixture; set aside.

3. Wrap stack of tortillas in damp paper towels; microwave on HIGH 1 minute or until warm. Spoon ¼ cup of the chicken mixture along center of each tortilla; roll up.

4. Arrange filled tortillas in 12- by 8-inch microwave-safe baking dish. Pour remaining soup mixture over tortillas. Cover with vented plastic wrap; microwave on HIGH 8 minutes or until heated through, rotating dish once during cooking.

5. Sprinkle with cheese. Microwave, uncovered, on HIGH 1 minute or until cheese is melted. Garnish with tomatoes, lettuce and olives. Makes 4 servings.

Chicken Tetrazzini

Here's a quick way to dress up leftover chicken or turkey for a
speedy meal any time.

1 can (10½ ounces) Franco-American Chicken Gravy
½ cup light cream
2 tablespoons dry sherry
1 tablespoon lemon juice
1 package (8 ounces) Campbell's Fresh Mushrooms,
    sliced
6 ounces spaghetti, cooked and drained
¼ cup chopped roasted red pepper or pimento
½ cup grated Parmesan cheese
1½ cups cubed cooked chicken or turkey

1. In 3-quart microwave-safe casserole, stir together gravy, cream, sherry and lemon juice. Cover with lid; microwave on HIGH 2 minutes or until hot.

2. Stir in mushrooms, spaghetti, red pepper and ¼ cup of the Parmesan. Stir in chicken. Cover; microwave on HIGH 7 minutes or until heated through, stirring once during cooking.

3. Top with remaining ¼ cup Parmesan. Microwave, uncovered, on HIGH 2 minutes. Let stand, uncovered, 2 minutes. Makes 4 servings.

Note: Substitute 2 cans (5 ounces each) Swanson Premium Chunk White Chicken, drained, for cubed cooked chicken.

TIP When you're grilling foods (such as burgers, ribs, chicken or hot dogs) outdoors, make each session count double. Cook twice as much food as you expect to eat, then freeze or refrigerate the remainder. Later, heat it in the microwave oven for food that tastes as if it just came off the grill.

Garden Chicken Salad

½ cup olive or vegetable oil
¼ cup red wine vinegar
 1 tablespoon Dijon-style mustard
 1 tablespoon finely chopped onion
 1 tablespoon chopped fresh parsley
¼ teaspoon salt
¼ teaspoon pepper
½ pound small potatoes
¼ pound green beans, trimmed
¼ cup water
 2 cans (5 ounces each) Swanson Premium Chunk White
    Chicken, drained
  Lettuce leaves
 2 hard-cooked eggs, sliced
 1 medium tomato, cut into wedges
  Pitted ripe olives for garnish

1. To prepare dressing: In small bowl or shaker jar, combine first 7 ingredients until well blended; set aside.

2. Pierce potatoes with fork in several places. Arrange potatoes in corners of 8- by 8-inch microwave-safe baking dish; arrange green beans in center. Add water. Cover with vented plastic wrap; microwave on HIGH 6 minutes or until vegetables are nearly tender, rearranging vegetables once during cooking. Let stand, covered, 5 minutes. Drain.

3. Cut potatoes into slices. In medium bowl, toss potatoes and beans with ¼ cup of the dressing. In another small bowl, toss chicken with 2 tablespoons of the dressing. Cover; chill if desired.

4. Arrange lettuce on platter. Mound chicken in center and arrange potatoes, beans, eggs and tomato wedges around chicken. Garnish with olives. Serve with remaining dressing. Makes 4 servings.

GARDEN CHICKEN SALAD ▶

Oriental Chicken Salad

2 tablespoons soy sauce
2 tablespoons orange juice
1 tablespoon rice wine vinegar
1 teaspoon sesame oil
1 cup carrots cut into matchstick-thin strips
¼ cup sweet red pepper cut into matchstick-thin strips
1 cup snow peas
3 cups shredded Chinese cabbage or lettuce
1 can (5 ounces) Swanson Premium Chunk White
   Chicken, drained
2 teaspoons toasted sesame seeds

1. In 1½-quart microwave-safe casserole, combine soy sauce, orange juice, vinegar and oil. Stir in carrots and pepper. Cover with lid; microwave on HIGH 2 minutes or until vegetables are softened. Stir in snow peas. Cover; microwave on HIGH 1 minute or until just heated through.

2. Divide cabbage between 2 salad plates; top with chicken. Spoon hot mixture over chicken. Sprinkle with sesame seeds. Makes 2 servings.

Note: To toast sesame seeds, spread 2 tablespoons sesame seeds on microwave-safe plate. Microwave, uncovered, on HIGH 2 minutes or until toasted, stirring once during cooking. Store extra toasted seeds in airtight container; use to sprinkle over vegetables, soups and salads.

Creamed Chicken in Patty Shells

½ cup chopped onion
1 can (11 ounces) Campbell's Condensed Cheddar
   Cheese Soup/Sauce or Nacho Cheese Soup/Dip
1 cup shredded Swiss cheese (4 ounces)
½ cup milk
3 tablespoons chopped pimento
1 tablespoon dry sherry
2 cans (5 ounces each) Swanson Premium Chunk White
   Chicken, drained
4 Pepperidge Farm Frozen Patty Shells, baked

1. Place onion in 2-quart microwave-safe casserole. Cover with lid; microwave on HIGH 1½ minutes or until tender.

2. Stir in soup until smooth. Stir in cheese, milk, pimento and sherry. Gently fold in chicken. Cover; microwave on HIGH 5 minutes or until hot and bubbling, stirring once during cooking. Serve over patty shells. Makes about 3 cups or 4 servings.

Orange-Chicken Timbales

These easy but sophisticated timbales make a delicious light lunch or supper for two.

1 can (5 ounces) Swanson Chunk Style Mixin' Chicken, undrained
1 egg
2 tablespoons fine dry bread crumbs
1 tablespoon finely chopped onion
1 tablespoon chopped fresh parsley
2 tablespoons plain yogurt
1 small clove garlic, minced
¼ teaspoon grated orange peel
Yogurt Sauce (recipe follows)

1. Butter two 6-ounce microwave-safe custard cups. In small bowl, thoroughly blend chicken with its liquid, egg, bread crumbs, onion, parsley, yogurt, garlic and orange peel. Press mixture firmly into prepared custard cups.

2. Cover with waxed paper; microwave at 50% power 4 minutes or until nearly set, rearranging cups once during cooking. Let stand, covered, while preparing Yogurt Sauce. Unmold onto plates; spoon sauce over. Makes 2 servings.

Yogurt Sauce: In small microwave-safe bowl, stir together ½ cup plain yogurt, 2 teaspoons honey, ⅛ teaspoon grated orange peel and dash ground nutmeg. Microwave, uncovered, on HIGH 30 seconds or until just warm. Makes ½ cup.

Mexicali Chicken Casserole

1 tablespoon butter or margarine
2 cups sliced Campbell's Fresh Mushrooms
½ cup chopped onion
1 can (11 ounces) Campbell's Condensed Nacho Cheese
    Soup/Dip
2 cups chopped cooked chicken
2 tomatoes, chopped
½ cup sour cream
1 cup shredded Cheddar cheese (4 ounces)
2 cups crushed tortilla chips

1. In 2-quart microwave-safe casserole, combine butter, mushrooms and onion. Cover with lid; microwave on HIGH 4 minutes or until vegetables are tender, stirring once during cooking.

2. Stir in soup until smooth; stir in chicken, tomatoes and sour cream. Cover; microwave on HIGH 4 minutes or until heated through, stirring once during cooking.

3. Spread ½ of the soup mixture into 10- by 6-inch microwave-safe baking dish. Sprinkle with ½ of the cheese and ½ of the chips. Spread remaining soup mixture over chips and sprinkle with remaining cheese. Cover with waxed paper; microwave on HIGH 4 minutes or until cheese is melted. Let stand, covered, 2 minutes. Sprinkle with remaining chips. Makes 6 servings.

Turkey Divan

1 pound broccoli, cut into spears, or 1 package
    (16 ounces) frozen broccoli spears
¼ cup water
1 can (10¾ ounces) Campbell's Condensed Cream of
    Mushroom Soup
¼ cup milk
1 tablespoon dry sherry
    Generous dash ground nutmeg
2 cups cubed cooked turkey or chicken
¼ cup shredded Cheddar cheese (1 ounce)

1. In 10- by 6-inch microwave-safe casserole, combine broccoli and water. Cover with vented plastic wrap; microwave on HIGH 6 minutes or until broccoli is almost tender, rotating dish once during cooking. Let stand, covered, 3 minutes. Drain.

2. In medium bowl, stir soup until smooth. Stir in milk, sherry and nutmeg; stir in turkey. Pour over broccoli. Sprinkle with cheese. Cover with waxed paper; microwave on HIGH 6 minutes or until heated through, rotating dish once during cooking. Let stand, covered, 5 minutes. Makes 4 servings.

Chicken Potato Topper

1 cup chopped carrots
½ cup thinly sliced celery
¼ cup chopped onion
1 tablespoon water
1 can (10¾ ounces) Campbell's Condensed Golden
     Mushroom Soup
⅓ cup milk
⅛ teaspoon pepper
⅛ teaspoon rubbed sage
1 can (5 ounces) Swanson Premium Chunk White
     Chicken, drained
3 hot baked potatoes, split
½ cup shredded Cheddar cheese (2 ounces)

1. In 1½-quart microwave-safe casserole, combine carrots, celery, onion and water. Cover with lid; microwave on HIGH 5 minutes or until vegetables are tender, stirring once during cooking.

2. Stir in soup, milk, pepper and sage. Cover; microwave on HIGH 3 minutes or until hot. Gently stir in chicken. Cover; microwave on HIGH 2 minutes or until hot and bubbling. Spoon chicken mixture over potatoes. Top with cheese. Makes 3 servings.

Note: To cook potatoes: Pierce 3 baking potatoes (8 ounces each) with fork in several places; arrange in circular pattern on microwave-safe plate. Microwave, uncovered, on HIGH 8 minutes or until tender, rearranging potatoes once during cooking. Let stand while preparing topper.

TIP   If you like baked potatoes better than microwaved ones, bake them in half the time. Pierce potatoes in several places, then cook in the microwave oven about half as long as you normally would. Finish baking them in the conventional oven at 400°F. 30 minutes or until tender.

Fish and Seafood

Salmon Steaks in Dill Sauce

- 1 tablespoon butter or margarine
- ½ cup chopped green onions
- 1 can (10¾ ounces) Campbell's Condensed Cream of Celery Soup
- ½ cup half-and-half
- ¼ cup Chablis or other dry white wine
- 2 tablespoons chopped fresh dill weed or 1 teaspoon dried dill weed, crushed
- 4 salmon steaks, ¾ inch thick (about 6 ounces each)

1. In 12- by 8-inch microwave-safe baking dish, combine butter and onions. Cover with vented plastic wrap; microwave on HIGH 2 minutes or until onions are tender, stirring once during cooking.

2. Stir in soup until smooth. Stir in half-and-half, wine and dill; blend well.

3. Arrange salmon steaks in sauce with thicker portions toward edges of dish. Cover; microwave on HIGH 9 minutes or until fish is nearly done, rotating dish twice during cooking. Let stand, covered, 5 minutes or until fish flakes easily with fork. Garnish with additional dill weed. Makes 4 servings.

SALMON STEAKS IN DILL SAUCE ▶

Mediterranean Cod

Serve this creamy fish in soup bowls accompanied with crusty French bread and a crisp green salad.

1 can (10¾ ounces) Campbell's Condensed Creamy
    Natural Potato Soup
¼ cup milk
2 green onions, thinly sliced
2 tablespoons lemon juice
2 teaspoons dry mustard
1 clove garlic, minced
1 package (10 ounces) Mrs. Paul's Frozen Buttered Fish
    Fillets
Chopped fresh parsley for garnish
Freshly ground pepper for garnish

1. In 8- by 8-inch microwave-safe baking dish, stir soup until smooth; stir in milk, onions, lemon juice, mustard and garlic until blended. Cover with vented plastic wrap; microwave on HIGH 3 minutes or until hot and bubbling, stirring once during cooking.

2. Arrange frozen fish fillets over sauce. Cover; microwave on HIGH 8 minutes or until fish flakes easily when tested with fork, rearranging fish and spooning sauce over once during cooking. Let stand, covered, 3 minutes. Garnish with parsley and pepper. Makes 2 servings.

Amandine Fish Fillets

1 package (10 ounces) Mrs. Paul's Frozen Au Naturel
    Haddock Fillets
2 tablespoons butter or margarine
½ cup chopped celery
½ cup shredded carrot
1 tablespoon chopped fresh parsley
¼ cup toasted sliced almonds (see Note on page 125)

1. Separate fish fillets, reserving seasoning packet. Set aside.

2. In small microwave-safe bowl, combine butter, celery and carrot. Cover with vented plastic wrap; microwave on HIGH 2 minutes or until vegetables are tender, stirring once during cooking.

3. Spread vegetables evenly in 12- by 8-inch microwave-safe baking dish; top with fish fillets, placing thicker portions toward edges of dish. Sprinkle with contents of seasoning packet. Cover with vented plastic wrap; microwave on HIGH 6 minutes or until fish is nearly done, rotating dish once during cooking. Let stand, covered, 5 minutes or until fish flakes easily with fork. Sprinkle with parsley and almonds. Makes 2 servings.

Crab-Stuffed Sole Fillets

**1 package (10 ounces) Mrs. Paul's Frozen Au Naturel Sole
    Fillets**
2 tablespoons butter or margarine
2 tablespoons chopped green onion
½ cup chopped Campbell's Fresh Mushrooms
¼ cup chopped celery
1 can (6 ounces) crabmeat, drained and picked over
**1 can (10¾ ounces) Campbell's Condensed Cream of
    Chicken or Cream of Celery Soup**
⅓ cup milk
2 tablespoons Chablis or other dry white wine
½ cup shredded Swiss cheese (2 ounces)

1. Separate fish fillets, reserving seasoning packet. Arrange fish on microwave-safe plate. Microwave, uncovered, on HIGH 1 minute or until fish is pliable. Set aside.

2. To make stuffing: In small microwave-safe bowl, combine butter, onion, mushrooms and celery. Cover with vented plastic wrap; microwave on HIGH 2 minutes or until vegetables are tender. Stir in crabmeat and 2 tablespoons of the soup. Make 4 mounds of stuffing in 10-inch microwave-safe pie plate. Divide fillets into 4 parts and arrange over stuffing; set aside.

3. In small microwave-safe bowl, stir remaining soup until smooth; stir in milk, wine, cheese and contents of seasoning packet. Microwave, uncovered, on HIGH 3 minutes or until cheese melts, stirring once during cooking.

4. Pour soup mixture over fish. Cover with waxed paper; microwave on HIGH 6 minutes or until fish is nearly done, rotating dish once during cooking. Let stand, covered, 5 minutes or until fish flakes easily with fork. Makes 4 servings.

TIP   If Mrs. Paul's Au Naturel Fish Fillets are not available in your supermarket, substitute an equal amount of fresh fish fillets. Omit thawing direction; other cooking times will be similar.

Snapper with Garden Vegetables

**1 whole red snapper (about 2 pounds), dressed, with
head and tail on**
1 tablespoon lime juice
1 tablespoon butter or margarine
½ cup celery cut into matchstick-thin strips
½ cup carrot cut into matchstick-thin strips
½ cup zucchini cut into matchstick-thin strips
**1 can (10¾ ounces) Campbell's Condensed Cream of
Celery Soup**
½ cup milk
1 clove garlic, minced
**2 tablespoons roasted red pepper or pimento cut into
strips**

1. Rinse fish; pat dry with paper towel. Pierce eyes with toothpick. Brush
fish inside and out with lime juice; set aside.

2. In medium microwave-safe bowl, combine butter, celery and carrot. Cover
with vented plastic wrap; microwave on HIGH 2 minutes. Stir in zucchini.
Cover; microwave 1 minute or until vegetables are tender-crisp. Stir ¼ cup of
the soup into vegetables.

3. Place fish on large microwave-safe platter. Spoon vegetables into cavity of
fish. Cover with vented plastic wrap; microwave at 50% power 20 minutes or
until fish flakes easily when tested with fork, rotating dish twice during
cooking. Let stand, covered, while preparing sauce.

4. To make sauce: In medium microwave-safe bowl, stir remaining soup until
smooth; stir in milk, garlic and red pepper. Cover with vented plastic wrap;
microwave on HIGH 3 minutes or until hot and bubbling, stirring once during
cooking. Spoon some sauce over fish; pass remainder. Makes 3 servings.

Note: Substitute two 1-pound fish for snapper. Divide vegetables between the
fish. Place both fish on large microwave-safe platter. Microwave as directed
above.

Note: Fish eyes will become cloudy. If desired, cover with halved grape or
olive slice after cooking.

TIP   Never put the twist ties that come with plastic storage
bags and some types of breads into the microwave oven. The
combination of wire and paper can cause arcing and could
ignite. For the same reason, don't put tea bags with metal
staples in your microwave oven.

SNAPPER WITH GARDEN VEGETABLES ▶

Lemony Stuffed Flounder

5 tablespoons butter or margarine
1/2 cup water
2 cups Pepperidge Farm Herb Seasoned Stuffing Mix
1/2 teaspoon grated lemon peel
1/2 cup chopped onion
1/2 cup shredded carrot
1 pound flounder fillets
Paprika for garnish
Lemon slices for garnish

1. In 4-cup glass measure, combine 4 tablespoons of the butter and water. Microwave, uncovered, on HIGH 1 1/2 minutes or until butter is melted. Stir in stuffing mix and lemon peel; set aside.

2. In 10-inch microwave-safe pie plate, combine remaining 1 tablespoon butter, onion and carrot. Cover with waxed paper; microwave on HIGH 3 minutes or until vegetables are tender, stirring once during cooking. Stir into stuffing mixture.

3. Make 4 mounds of stuffing in same pie plate. Divide fish into 4 parts and arrange over stuffing. Sprinkle with paprika and top with lemon slices. Cover with waxed paper; microwave on HIGH 8 minutes or until fish is nearly done, rotating dish once during cooking. Let stand, covered, 5 minutes or until fish flakes easily when tested with fork. Makes 4 servings.

Tuna-Pasta Casserole

1 cup frozen peas
1 can (10 3/4 ounces) Campbell's Condensed Cream of Celery Soup
1/2 cup milk
1/2 cup shredded Swiss cheese (2 ounces)
1 can (6 1/2 ounces) tuna, drained and flaked
2 cups cooked corkscrew or other macaroni (1 cup uncooked)
2 hard-cooked eggs, chopped
1/2 cup crushed potato chips

1. Place peas in small microwave-safe bowl. Cover with vented plastic wrap; microwave on HIGH 4 minutes or until tender. Drain; set aside.

2. In 1 1/2-quart microwave-safe casserole, stir soup until smooth; stir in milk and cheese. Fold tuna, macaroni, eggs and peas into soup mixture. Cover with lid; microwave on HIGH 7 minutes or until hot and bubbling, stirring once during cooking. Let stand, covered, 5 minutes.

3. Sprinkle potato chips over casserole. Makes 4 servings.

Salmon and Spinach Pie

For maximum calcium value, don't remove the bones from the salmon; just mash them with the fish. The soft bones will blend well with the rest of the dish.

1 can (15½ ounces) salmon, drained and flaked
⅓ cup fine dry bread crumbs
1 tablespoon lemon juice
⅛ teaspoon pepper
1 can (10¾ ounces) Campbell's Condensed Cream of
**   Celery Soup**
3 eggs
1 package (10 ounces) frozen chopped spinach, thawed
**   and well drained (see Note on page 54)**
¼ teaspoon ground nutmeg

1. In medium bowl, thoroughly mix salmon, crumbs, lemon juice, pepper, ⅓ cup of the soup and 1 of the eggs. Spread evenly in 9-inch microwave-safe pie plate. Cover with waxed paper; microwave on HIGH 3 minutes or until hot, rotating dish once during cooking.

2. Meanwhile, in same bowl, stir remaining soup until smooth; stir in remaining 2 eggs, spinach and nutmeg. Spread evenly over salmon mixture.

3. Elevate if necessary (see page 7). Microwave, uncovered, at 50% power 20 minutes or until center is set, rotating dish twice during cooking. Let stand, uncovered, 5 minutes. Makes 6 servings.

TIP   Bake an entire package of brown-and-serve rolls in your conventional oven, even if you won't use them all at once. Wrap and freeze leftovers. Later, warm just what you need in the microwave oven.

Orange-Ginger Fish

1 package (10 ounces) Mrs. Paul's Frozen Au Naturel
    Haddock or Cod Fillets
1 tablespoon butter or margarine
1/2 teaspoon grated orange peel
2 tablespoons orange juice
1 teaspoon teriyaki sauce
1 teaspoon chopped chives
1/8 teaspoon grated fresh ginger

1. Arrange fish fillets in 12- by 8-inch microwave-safe baking dish, placing thicker portions toward edges of dish; reserve seasoning packet. Set aside.

2. Place butter in small microwave-safe bowl. Cover; microwave on HIGH 20 seconds or until melted. Stir in orange peel, orange juice, teriyaki sauce, chives and ginger; pour over fish. Sprinkle with contents of seasoning packet.

3. Cover with vented plastic wrap; microwave on HIGH 6 minutes or until fish is nearly done, rotating dish once during cooking. Let stand, covered, 5 minutes or until fish flakes easily with fork. Makes 2 servings.

Note: If fish is not done after standing time, microwave, covered, 1 to 2 minutes more, checking fish every 30 seconds.

Scallops in Cream Sauce

1 tablespoon butter or margarine
1 cup sliced Campbell's Fresh Mushrooms
2 tablespoons sliced green onion
1 clove garlic, minced
1 can (10¾ ounces) Campbell's Condensed Cream of
    Celery Soup
1 pound bay scallops or halved sea scallops
2 tablespoons Chablis or other dry white wine
4 teaspoons grated Parmesan cheese
    Paprika for garnish

1. In 1½-quart microwave-safe casserole, combine butter, mushrooms, green onion and garlic. Cover with lid; microwave on HIGH 3 minutes or until vegetables are tender, stirring once during cooking.

2. Stir in soup until smooth. Stir in scallops and wine. Microwave, uncovered, on HIGH 10 minutes or until scallops are opaque, stirring twice during cooking. Let stand, uncovered, 2 minutes. Divide among 4 individual casseroles or shells; sprinkle with cheese and paprika. Makes 4 servings.

ORANGE-GINGER FISH ▶

Jambalaya

2 tablespoons olive oil or bacon drippings
1 cup chopped onion
1 cup chopped green pepper
1 large clove garlic, minced
½ pound skinless boneless raw chicken, cut into 1-inch
        pieces
¼ pound smoked sausage, cut into ½-inch pieces
½ cup regular long-grain rice, uncooked
1½ cups "V8" Vegetable Juice
2 tablespoons Louisiana-style hot sauce or 1 teaspoon
        hot pepper sauce
¼ teaspoon dried thyme leaves, crushed
1 bay leaf
½ pound medium shrimp, shelled and deveined
¼ cup chopped fresh parsley

1. In 3-quart microwave-safe casserole, combine oil, onion, green pepper and garlic. Cover with lid; microwave on HIGH 4 minutes or until vegetables are tender, stirring once during cooking.

2. Stir in chicken, sausage, rice, "V8" juice, hot sauce, thyme and bay leaf. Cover; microwave on HIGH 10 minutes or until bubbling, stirring once during cooking. Stir again.

3. Reduce power to 50%. Cover; microwave 10 minutes or until rice is nearly done. Stir in shrimp and parsley. Cover; microwave at 50% power 5 minutes or until most shrimp are opaque, stirring once during cooking. Let stand, covered, 5 minutes or until all shrimp are opaque. Remove bay leaf. Makes about 6 cups or 6 servings.

TIP When a food container is described as "microwave-only," never put it in a conventional oven, not even to keep the food warm at a very low setting. These containers can melt or scorch at very low temperatures. (The same applies to microwave-only cookware.)

Simple Shrimp Creole

    1 tablespoon butter or margarine
  ½ cup chopped onion
    1 medium green pepper, cut into matchstick-thin strips
  ½ cup thinly sliced celery
1¾ cups Prego al Fresco Spaghetti Sauce
  ¾ pound medium shrimp, shelled and deveined
    1 bay leaf
  ⅛ teaspoon pepper
    Generous dash hot pepper sauce
    Hot cooked rice

1. In 2-quart microwave-safe casserole, combine butter, onion, green pepper and celery. Cover with lid; microwave on HIGH 4 minutes or until vegetables are tender, stirring once during cooking.

2. Stir in spaghetti sauce, shrimp, bay leaf, pepper and hot pepper sauce. Cover; microwave on HIGH 6 minutes or until most shrimp are opaque, stirring once during cooking. Let stand, covered, 5 minutes or until all shrimp are opaque. Remove bay leaf. Serve over rice. Makes about 5 cups or 4 servings.

Shrimp Fettucini

  ½ cup carrot cut into matchstick-thin strips
  ½ cup celery cut into matchstick-thin strips
    2 cloves garlic, minced
  ½ teaspoon dried dill weed, crushed
    1 can (10¾ ounces) Campbell's Condensed Creamy
      Onion Soup/Dip
  ½ cup milk
  ½ pound medium shrimp, shelled and deveined
    6 ounces fettucini, cooked and drained
  ⅓ cup grated Parmesan cheese
    1 tablespoon lemon juice

1. In 3-quart microwave-safe casserole, combine carrot, celery, garlic and dill. Cover with lid; microwave on HIGH 3 minutes or until vegetables are tender-crisp, stirring once during cooking.

2. Stir in soup until smooth. Stir in milk, shrimp, fettucini, Parmesan and lemon juice. Cover; microwave at 50% power 15 minutes or until most shrimp are opaque, stirring twice during cooking. Let stand, covered, 5 minutes or until all shrimp are opaque. Makes about 5 cups or 4 servings.

Fish Stew

1 package (10 ounces) Mrs. Paul's Frozen Au Naturel Cod
      Fillets
1 cup sliced celery
1 can (14½ ounces) Swanson Clear Ready to Serve
      Chicken Broth
1 jar (15½ ounces) Prego Spaghetti Sauce
12 mussels, well scrubbed, or ½ pound scallops
½ pound medium shrimp, shelled and deveined

1. Separate fish fillets, reserving seasoning packet. Arrange fish on microwave-safe plate. Microwave, uncovered, on HIGH 1 minute or until fish is pliable. Cut fish into 1-inch pieces; set aside.

2. In 3-quart microwave-safe casserole, combine celery and ¼ cup of the broth. Cover with lid; microwave on HIGH 3 minutes or until celery is tender, stirring once during cooking.

3. Stir in spaghetti sauce, remaining broth and contents of seasoning packet. Cover; microwave on HIGH 5 minutes or until very hot.

4. Add fish, mussels and shrimp. Cover; microwave on HIGH 8 minutes or until fish flakes easily with fork and most mussels are open. Discard any unopened mussels. Makes about 6 cups or 4 servings.

Pasta with Clam Sauce

1 can (10¾ ounces) Campbell's Condensed Cream of
      Mushroom or Cream of Celery Soup
1 can (6½ ounces) minced clams, undrained
¼ cup milk
¼ cup Chablis or other dry white wine
2 tablespoons chopped fresh parsley
2 tablespoons grated Parmesan cheese
1 large clove garlic, minced
8 ounces linguini, cooked and drained

1. In 1½-quart microwave-safe casserole, stir soup until smooth; stir in clams with their liquid, milk, wine, parsley, Parmesan and garlic. Cover with lid; microwave on HIGH 8 minutes or until hot and bubbling, stirring once during cooking.

2. Toss with linguini; serve with additional Parmesan. Makes 4 servings.

FISH STEW ▶

Beef, Pork and Lamb

Chili Burritos

This zesty filling mixture also makes wonderful sandwiches when served on hamburger rolls.

   1 pound ground beef
 ¼ cup chopped green pepper
   1 can (11 ounces) Campbell's Condensed Zesty Tomato
        Soup/Sauce
   1 tablespoon chili powder
   1 tablespoon Worcestershire sauce
   8 flour tortillas (8-inch)
        Guacamole, chopped tomatoes and shredded Cheddar
        cheese for garnish

1. Crumble beef into 2-quart microwave-safe casserole; stir in green pepper. Cover with lid; microwave on HIGH 5 minutes or until beef is no longer pink, stirring once during cooking to break up meat. Spoon off fat.

2. Stir in soup, chili powder and Worcestershire. Cover; microwave on HIGH 5 minutes or until hot and bubbling.

3. Wrap stack of tortillas in damp paper towels. Microwave on HIGH 1 minute or until warm. Spoon heaping ¼ cup meat mixture onto each tortilla. Fold in sides and roll up to make burritos. Garnish with guacamole, tomatoes and cheese. Makes 8 burritos or 4 servings.

CHILI BURRITOS ▶

Souper Pot Roast

*You can also use cream of celery soup or creamy onion soup/dip
to make delicious pot roasts.*

2 tablespoons all-purpose flour
2½- to 3-pound beef chuck roast
**1 can (10¾ ounces) Campbell's Condensed Cream of
   Mushroom Soup**
1 bay leaf
4 carrots, peeled and cut into 2-inch lengths
2 large potatoes, cut into quarters

1. Place flour in 3-quart microwave-safe casserole. Add roast, turning to coat
with flour on all sides; discard excess flour. Spread soup over meat; add bay
leaf. Cover with lid; microwave on HIGH 20 minutes.

2. Turn roast over, spooning soup over roast. Reduce power to 50%. Cover;
microwave 20 minutes.

3. Add carrots and potatoes to casserole. Cover; microwave at 50% power
40 minutes or until meat and vegetables are tender, rotating dish once during
cooking. Let stand, covered, 10 minutes. Remove bay leaf. Makes 6 servings.

Note: The shape of a pot roast can make a big difference in the time needed
for cooking it (this is also true for conventional cooking methods). Choose a
flatter roast for quicker, more even cooking; a cube-shaped roast will require
more time.

TIP To reheat leftover roast beef, turkey or other cooked
meats in Franco-American Beef, Chicken or Mushroom Gravy:
In 2-quart microwave-safe casserole, pour 1 can (10½ ounces)
gravy over about 1 pound sliced, cooked meat. Cover with lid;
microwave on HIGH 3 minutes or until heated through,
rotating dish once during cooking. This is also a great way to
make hot roast beef or turkey sandwiches.

Vegetable-Stuffed Flank Steak

1 tablespoon olive or vegetable oil
1 cup chopped Campbell's Fresh Mushrooms
1 package (10 ounces) frozen chopped spinach, thawed
  and drained (see Note on page 54)
1/2 cup chopped onion
1 clove garlic, minced
1 cup shredded carrots
1/2 cup shredded Muenster or Swiss cheese (2 ounces)
1/2 teaspoon dried basil leaves, crushed
1/8 teaspoon pepper
1 1/2 pounds beef flank steak, pounded to 1/4-inch thickness
1 can (10 3/4 ounces) Campbell's Condensed Creamy
  Onion Soup/Dip or Cream of Mushroom Soup
2 tablespoons dry sherry

1. In 1 1/2-quart microwave-safe casserole, combine oil, mushrooms, spinach, onion and garlic. Cover with lid; microwave on HIGH 5 minutes or until vegetables are tender, stirring once during cooking. Drain. Stir in carrots, cheese, basil and pepper; mix well.

2. Spread vegetable mixture over steak to within 1 inch of edges. Roll up from long end, jelly-roll fashion, tucking ends of steak into roll. Secure with wooden toothpicks or tie with cotton string. Place seam-side down in 12- by 8-inch microwave-safe baking dish.

3. In small bowl, stir soup until smooth; stir in sherry. Pour over meat. Cover with vented plastic wrap; microwave on HIGH 10 minutes, rotating dish once during cooking.

4. Spoon pan juices over meat. Reduce power to 50%. Cover; microwave 20 minutes or until meat is tender, rotating dish twice during cooking. Let stand, covered, 10 minutes. Makes 6 servings.

Beef Ragoût

1 tablespoon butter or margarine
1/2 cup chopped onion
1 large clove garlic, minced
1 pound beef for stew, cut into 1-inch pieces
1 cup thinly sliced carrots
1 can (10 1/4 ounces) Franco-American Beef Gravy
1/4 cup Burgundy or other dry red wine
1/4 cup tomato paste
   Hot cooked noodles

1. In 2-quart microwave-safe casserole, combine butter, onion and garlic. Cover with lid; microwave on HIGH 3 minutes or until onion is tender, stirring once during cooking.

2. Stir in beef. Cover; microwave on HIGH 5 minutes or until beef is no longer pink, stirring once during cooking.

3. Stir in carrots, gravy, wine and tomato paste. Cover; microwave on HIGH 5 minutes or until boiling. Stir again.

4. Reduce power to 50%. Cover; microwave 30 minutes or until meat is tender, stirring twice during cooking. Let stand, covered, 5 minutes. Serve over noodles. Makes about 3 cups or 4 servings.

Note: It's often more economical to buy a chuck steak or roast and cut your own stew meat than to buy "beef for stew." You usually have to trim the market-cut meat anyway, and you can control the size of the pieces better when you cut it yourself.

TIP   If you're saving leftovers in the freezer for reheating in the microwave, freeze them in single-serving portions. Then you can remove exactly the number of portions you need and they'll reheat more quickly and evenly than if you had three or four portions frozen together. You can put the small portions in sandwich bags, then place small bags in a larger freezer bag.

Ginger Beef

¾ pound beef flank steak
1 can (11 ounces) Campbell's Condensed Zesty Tomato
   Soup/Sauce
⅓ cup water
 2 tablespoons peanut or vegetable oil
 1 tablespoon soy sauce
 2 teaspoons grated fresh ginger or ½ teaspoon ground
   ginger
 1 clove garlic, minced
 1 medium green pepper, cut into 1-inch squares
 1 cup broccoli flowerets
   Hot cooked rice

1. Freeze steak 1 hour to make slicing easier. Cut steak across the grain into very thin slices.

2. In 12- by 8-inch microwave-safe baking dish, stir together soup, water, oil, soy sauce, ginger and garlic. Add beef slices; toss to coat well. Cover; refrigerate at least 1 hour.

3. Cover with vented plastic wrap; microwave on HIGH 6 minutes or until beef is no longer pink, stirring twice during cooking.

4. Add green pepper and broccoli. Cover; microwave on HIGH 5 minutes or until vegetables are tender, stirring twice during cooking. Serve over rice. Makes about 3½ cups or 4 servings.

TIP   Use window cleaner to clean inside surfaces of your microwave oven; it removes most food spatters and odors, too.

Shepherd's Pie

For a festive touch, use a pastry tube to pipe the mashed potatoes around the edge of the dish.

> 1 tablespoon butter or margarine
> 1 cup thinly sliced carrots
> ½ cup chopped onion
> 1 can (10¼ ounces) Franco-American Beef Gravy
> 1½ cups cubed cooked beef
> 2 cups hot mashed potatoes or Microwave Mashed
>   Potatoes (recipe follows)
> ¼ cup shredded Cheddar cheese (1 ounce)

1. In 2-quart microwave-safe casserole, combine butter, carrots and onion. Cover with lid; microwave on HIGH 5 minutes or until vegetables are nearly tender, stirring once during cooking.

2. Stir in gravy and beef. Cover; microwave on HIGH 5 minutes or until bubbling, stirring once during cooking.

3. Spoon potatoes around edge of casserole; sprinkle with cheese. Microwave, uncovered, on HIGH 3 minutes or until cheese is melted. Makes 4 servings.

Note: Substitute 1 pound ground beef, cooked and drained, for the cubed cooked beef.

Microwave Mashed Potatoes: Pierce 3 medium potatoes (1 pound) with fork in several places; arrange in circular pattern on microwave-safe plate. Microwave, uncovered, on HIGH 7 minutes or until tender, rearranging potatoes once during cooking. Scoop potato pulp from skins, discarding skins. In medium bowl, combine potato pulp, ¼ cup milk, 1 tablespoon butter or margarine and ¼ teaspoon salt. With electric mixer or potato masher, mash until smooth.

TIP   If you don't have leftover mashed potatoes on hand and don't feel like mashing some, turn to packaged instant mashed potatoes. You'll find microwave preparation directions on the package.

SHEPHERD'S PIE ▶

Zesty Meat Loaf

1½ **pounds lean ground beef**
   1 **can (11 ounces) Campbell's Condensed Zesty Tomato
      Soup/Sauce**
   2 **eggs, beaten**
 ¾ **cup finely crushed saltines**
   1 **tablespoon Worcestershire sauce**
   2 **tablespoons grated Parmesan cheese**

1. In large bowl, thoroughly blend beef, ½ cup of the soup, eggs, crumbs and Worcestershire sauce.

2. In 12- by 8-inch microwave-safe baking dish, firmly shape meat mixture into 8- by 4-inch loaf. Cover with waxed paper; microwave on HIGH 15 minutes or until loaf is firm in center, rotating dish twice during cooking.

3. Spread remaining soup over meat. Microwave, uncovered, on HIGH 2 minutes or until soup is hot. Top with cheese. Let stand, uncovered, 5 minutes. Makes 6 servings.

Note: If you are using a temperature probe, cook meat loaf to an internal temperature of 145° to 150°F.

Tavern Chili

   1 **pound ground beef**
   2 **tablespoons chili powder**
   1 **clove garlic, minced**
   1 **pouch Campbell's Onion Mushroom Soup and Recipe
      Mix**
 ¾ **cup beer or water**
   1 **can (14½ ounces) tomatoes, undrained, cut up**
   1 **can (about 15 ounces) kidney beans, drained**
      Shredded Cheddar cheese for garnish
      Sour cream for garnish

1. Crumble beef into 2-quart microwave-safe casserole; stir in chili powder and garlic. Cover with lid; microwave on HIGH 5 minutes or until beef is no longer pink, stirring once during cooking to break up meat. Spoon off fat.

2. Stir in soup mix, beer, tomatoes with their liquid and beans. Cover; microwave on HIGH 3 minutes or until hot and bubbling. Stir again.

3. Reduce power to 50%. Cover; microwave 10 minutes or until flavors are well blended, stirring once during cooking. Let stand, covered, 5 minutes. Garnish with cheese and sour cream. Makes about 5 cups or 5 servings.

Picadillo-Stuffed Peppers

For an especially attractive presentation, stuff two green and two red peppers.

4 medium green or sweet red peppers
1 tablespoon water
1 pound lean ground beef
½ cup chopped onion
1 clove garlic, minced
½ teaspoon ground cinnamon
½ teaspoon ground cumin
⅛ teaspoon ground cloves
1 can (11 ounces) Campbell's Condensed Zesty Tomato Soup/Sauce
1 small apple, chopped
¼ cup raisins
¼ cup toasted sliced almonds (see Note on page 125)
1 tablespoon vinegar

1. Cut thin slice from top of each pepper. Chop enough pepper tops to make ⅓ cup; set aside. Remove and discard inner membranes and seeds from peppers. Place pepper shells in 2-quart microwave-safe casserole; add water. Cover with lid; microwave on HIGH 5 minutes or until tender-crisp. Drain and set aside.

2. Crumble beef into same casserole; add onion, garlic, cinnamon, cumin, cloves and chopped pepper tops. Cover; microwave on HIGH 5 minutes or until beef is no longer pink, stirring once during cooking to break up meat. Spoon off fat.

3. Stir in soup, apple, raisins, almonds and vinegar. Divide mixture among peppers. Arrange in 2-quart microwave-safe casserole. Cover; microwave on HIGH 5 minutes or until hot. Makes 4 servings.

Vegetable-Stuffed Meat Cups

1 package (10 ounces) frozen mixed vegetables
1 cup shredded Swiss cheese (4 ounces)
1½ pounds ground beef
   1 pouch Campbell's Onion Soup and Recipe Mix
   1 egg
   ½ cup fresh bread crumbs
   2 tablespoons ketchup

1. Place vegetables in small microwave-safe bowl. Cover with vented plastic wrap; microwave on HIGH 3½ minutes or until tender-crisp. Drain. Add ½ cup of the cheese; toss to mix well. Set aside.

2. In large bowl, combine beef, soup mix, egg, bread crumbs and ketchup; mix well. Divide meat mixture into 8 equal parts. Press into bottoms and up sides of eight 6-ounce custard cups or individual casseroles. Divide vegetable mixture among meat cups.

3. Arrange 4 custard cups in a circle in the microwave oven. Microwave, uncovered, on HIGH 4 minutes or until meat is no longer pink, rearranging cups once during cooking. Sprinkle each with 1 tablespoon of the remaining cheese. Let stand, covered, while cooking remaining cups.

4. Repeat step 3 with remaining meat cups. Makes 8 servings.

Note: For more substantial servings, divide meat mixture among six 10-ounce custard cups or casseroles. Continue as directed in steps 2 and 3, but cook all 6 cups at once on HIGH for 8 minutes, rearranging cups once during cooking. Makes 6 servings.

Korean Beef in Lettuce

Hoisin sauce is a sweet, spicy Oriental seasoning sauce made from soybeans, garlic and spices. You can find it in Oriental markets and many supermarkets.

10 romaine lettuce leaves
2 tablespoons water
1 pound ground beef
1 pouch Campbell's Onion Soup and Recipe Mix
1 package (8 ounces) Campbell's Fresh Mushrooms, chopped
¼ cup hoisin sauce
1 tablespoon dry sherry or rice wine
2 teaspoons cornstarch
1½ cups warm cooked rice

1. Arrange romaine leaves in 12- by 8-inch microwave-safe baking dish; add water. Cover with vented plastic wrap; microwave on HIGH 3 minutes or until wilted. Drain and set aside.

2. Crumble beef into 2-quart microwave-safe casserole. Cover with lid; microwave on HIGH 5 minutes or until beef is no longer pink, stirring once during cooking to break up meat. Spoon off fat.

3. Stir in soup mix, mushrooms and hoisin sauce. In cup, stir together sherry and cornstarch; stir into meat mixture. Cover; microwave on HIGH 5 minutes or until very hot, stirring once during cooking.

4. Lay drained lettuce leaves on counter. Mound 2 heaping tablespoons of rice in center of each; top with about ¼ cup of the meat mixture. Fold in sides and roll up to form bundles. Makes 10 rolls or 5 servings.

TIP Cook ground beef or bulk sausage in a microwave-safe colander set in a larger bowl or casserole. The fat will drain off the meat during cooking.

Stuffed Cabbage

6 cabbage leaves
½ cup water
1 pound ground beef or pork
1 cup cooked rice
½ cup chopped onion
1 egg
1 tablespoon Worcestershire sauce
⅛ teaspoon pepper
1 can (10¾ ounces) Campbell's Condensed Tomato Soup
2 teaspoons vinegar

1. Arrange cabbage leaves in 3-quart microwave-safe casserole; add water. Cover with lid; microwave on HIGH 6 minutes or until soft, rotating dish once during cooking. Drain and set aside.

2. In medium bowl, thoroughly mix beef, rice, onion, egg, Worcestershire, pepper and 2 tablespoons of the soup.

3. Lay drained cabbage leaves on counter. Spoon about ½ cup of the meat mixture onto each cabbage leaf. Fold in sides and roll up to form bundles; secure with wooden toothpicks if necessary. Arrange in same casserole.

4. In small bowl, stir together remaining soup and vinegar. Spoon over cabbage rolls. Cover with lid; microwave on HIGH 15 minutes or until meat is cooked and cabbage is tender, rotating dish once during cooking. Let stand, covered, 5 minutes. Makes 6 servings.

TIP Many frozen foods are packaged in paperboard containers for conventional or microwave heating. Once these paperboard containers have been heated, they cannot be reused. They are intended for only one heating. The sturdy plastic plates used in products such as Le Menu Frozen Dinners may be reused in the microwave oven.

Veal Stew

1 pound veal for stew, cut into ½-inch pieces
1 tablespoon all-purpose flour
1 can (10½ ounces) Campbell's Chunky Creamy
    Mushroom Soup
1 cup frozen baby carrots or fresh carrots cut into sticks
½ cup fresh or frozen pearl onions
¼ teaspoon dried thyme leaves, crushed
1 teaspoon lemon juice

1. In 3-quart microwave-safe casserole, stir together veal and flour. Cover with lid; microwave on HIGH 5 minutes or until veal is no longer pink, stirring once during cooking.

2. Stir soup into meat mixture until smooth. Stir in carrots, onions and thyme. Cover; microwave at 50% power 25 minutes or until veal is tender, stirring 3 times during cooking. Stir in lemon juice. Let stand, covered, 5 minutes. Makes about 3½ cups or 4 servings.

Beef Stroganoff

1 pound boneless beef sirloin steak
½ cup chopped onion
1 can (10¾ ounces) Campbell's Condensed Cream of
    Mushroom Soup
½ cup sour cream
½ teaspoon paprika
    Hot cooked noodles

1. Freeze steak 1 hour to make slicing easier. Cut steak across the grain into very thin slices.

2. In 2-quart microwave-safe casserole, combine beef and onion. Cover with lid; microwave on HIGH 5 minutes or until beef is no longer pink, stirring once during cooking.

3. In small bowl, stir soup until smooth; stir in sour cream and paprika. Add to beef, stirring to coat. Cover; microwave at 50% power 3 minutes or until heated through. Serve over noodles. Makes about 3½ cups or 4 servings.

Spicy Chili Verde

Serve this flavorful stew with chili beans for an authentic Western meal.

1½ pounds pork for stew, cut into ½-inch pieces
⅓ cup all-purpose flour
¾ cup chopped green pepper
½ cup chopped onion
1 can (4 ounces) chopped green chilies, drained
1 can (11 ounces) Campbell's Condensed Zesty Tomato Soup/Sauce
1 can (10½ ounces) Campbell's Condensed Beef Consommé
1 cup water
1 tablespoon lemon juice
2 cloves garlic, minced
1 bay leaf
1 teaspoon dried oregano leaves, crushed
¼ teaspoon ground cumin
⅛ teaspoon ground cloves
Hot cooked rice

1. In 3-quart microwave-safe casserole, toss pork with flour to coat. Stir in green pepper and onion. Cover with lid; microwave on HIGH 8 minutes, stirring once during cooking.

2. Stir in remaining ingredients except rice. Cover; microwave on HIGH 8 minutes or until bubbling, stirring once during cooking.

3. Reduce power to 50%. Cover; microwave 45 minutes or until pork is tender, stirring 3 times during cooking. Let stand, covered, 5 minutes. Remove bay leaf. Serve over rice. Makes about 6 cups or 6 servings.

Oriental Pork

1 teaspoon sesame oil
1 teaspoon vegetable oil
1 teaspoon grated fresh ginger
1 tablespoon soy sauce
1 tablespoon dry sherry
1 clove garlic, minced
1 pound boneless pork, cut into 2- by ¼-inch strips
1 can (10½ ounces) Campbell's Condensed Beef Broth
    (Bouillon)
2 tablespoons cornstarch
1 cup snow peas
1 sweet red pepper, cut into strips
1 cup sliced Campbell's Fresh Mushrooms

1. In 3-quart microwave-safe casserole, stir together oils, ginger, soy sauce, sherry and garlic. Stir in pork to coat. Cover with lid; refrigerate 1 hour.

2. Microwave, covered, on HIGH 5 minutes or until pork is no longer pink, stirring once during cooking.

3. In small bowl, stir together broth and cornstarch; add to pork mixture along with peas, pepper and mushrooms. Cover; microwave on HIGH 7 minutes or until hot and bubbling, stirring 3 times during cooking. Serve over hot cooked rice, if desired. Makes about 5 cups or 5 servings.

Barbecued Spareribs

1 pouch Campbell's Onion Soup and Recipe Mix
½ cup water
½ cup ketchup
¼ cup packed brown sugar
2 tablespoons vinegar
1 teaspoon chili powder
¼ teaspoon hot pepper sauce
2½ pounds pork spareribs, cut into individual ribs

1. To prepare sauce, in small bowl, stir together soup mix, water, ketchup, brown sugar, vinegar, chili powder and hot pepper sauce. Arrange ribs in 12- by 8-inch microwave-safe baking dish, placing thicker portions toward edges of dish. Pour sauce over ribs. Cover with vented plastic wrap; microwave on HIGH 5 minutes. Rearrange ribs.

2. Reduce power to 50%. Cover; microwave 40 minutes or until ribs are tender, rearranging ribs and spooning off fat twice during cooking. Let stand, covered, 5 minutes. Spoon off fat. Makes 4 servings.

ORIENTAL PORK ▶

Sweet and Sour Pork

1 pound boneless pork, cut into 1-inch pieces
1 clove garlic, minced
1 can (10½ ounces) Campbell's Condensed Beef
    Consommé
2 tablespoons brown sugar
2 tablespoons vinegar
1 green pepper, cut into strips
1 sweet red pepper, cut into strips
3 tablespoons cornstarch
2 tablespoons soy sauce
1 can (20 ounces) pineapple chunks, drained
    Hot cooked rice

1. In 2-quart microwave-safe casserole, combine pork and garlic. Cover with lid; microwave on HIGH 6 minutes or until pork is no longer pink, stirring once during cooking. Spoon off any excess liquid.

2. Stir in consommé, brown sugar, vinegar and peppers. Cover; microwave on HIGH 5 minutes or until boiling, stirring twice during cooking.

3. In cup, stir together cornstarch and soy sauce. Stir into casserole. Stir in pineapple. Cover; microwave on HIGH 3 minutes or until sauce is thickened, stirring once during cooking. Let stand, covered, 3 minutes. Serve over rice. Makes about 5 cups or 5 servings.

Two-Bean Franks

½ cup chopped onion
½ cup chopped celery
1 clove garlic, minced
2 cans (16 ounces each) Campbell's Pork & Beans in
    Tomato Sauce
1 can (about 15 ounces) kidney beans, drained
5 frankfurters, sliced
¼ teaspoon dry mustard

1. In 3-quart microwave-safe casserole, combine onion, celery and garlic. Cover with lid; microwave on HIGH 3 minutes or until vegetables are tender, stirring once during cooking.

2. Stir in remaining ingredients. Cover; microwave on HIGH 10 minutes or until hot and bubbling, stirring twice during cooking. Let stand, covered, 5 minutes. Makes about 6 cups or 5 servings.

Pork Chops and Sauerkraut

2 slices bacon, chopped
½ cup chopped onion
1 jar (32 ounces) Vlasic Polish Sauerkraut, rinsed and
**   drained**
2 apples, peeled and chopped
¼ teaspoon pepper
4 medium pork chops (about 1½ pounds)

1. In 3-quart microwave-safe casserole, combine bacon and onion. Cover with lid; microwave on HIGH 3½ minutes or until bacon is crisp and onion is tender, stirring once during cooking.

2. Stir in sauerkraut, apples and pepper. Arrange pork chops over sauerkraut, placing thicker portions toward edge of dish. Cover; microwave on HIGH 8 minutes or until very hot. Rearrange pork chops.

3. Reduce power to 50%. Cover; microwave 20 minutes or until pork is no longer pink in center, rearranging chops once during cooking. Let stand, covered, 5 minutes. Makes 4 servings.

Lamb Stew

1½ pounds boneless lamb, cut into ½-inch pieces
1 can (10½ ounces) Franco-American Mushroom Gravy
4 small potatoes, cut into quarters
1 tablespoon chopped fresh mint leaves or 1 teaspoon
**   dried mint leaves, crushed**
1 cup frozen peas
1 cup quartered Campbell's Fresh Mushrooms
1 tablespoon lemon juice

1. Place lamb in 3-quart microwave-safe casserole. Cover with lid; microwave on HIGH 6 minutes or until lamb is no longer pink, stirring once during cooking. Spoon off fat.

2. Stir in gravy, potatoes and mint. Cover; microwave on HIGH 5 minutes or until bubbling. Stir again.

3. Reduce power to 50%. Cover; microwave 20 minutes or until meat is nearly tender, stirring twice during cooking.

4. Stir in peas, mushrooms and lemon juice. Cover; microwave at 50% power 10 minutes or until vegetables and meat are tender, stirring once during cooking. Let stand, covered, 5 minutes. Makes about 6 cups or 6 servings.

Lamb Curry

Add tomatoes for a more robust flavor and color; leave them out for creamier curry.

1 tablespoon butter or margarine
1 cup chopped onion
2 tablespoons curry powder
1½ pounds boneless lamb, cut into ½-inch pieces
¼ cup all-purpose flour
1 cup Swanson Clear Ready to Serve Chicken Broth
2 apples, peeled and chopped
1 can (8 ounces) tomatoes, drained and cut up (optional)
¼ cup chutney
½ cup sour cream or plain yogurt
Chopped peanuts for garnish
Hot cooked rice

1. In 3-quart microwave-safe casserole, combine butter, onion and curry. Cover with lid; microwave on HIGH 4 minutes or until onion is tender, stirring once during cooking.

2. In large bowl, toss lamb with flour. Stir lamb and flour into casserole. Cover; microwave on HIGH 6 minutes or until meat is no longer pink, stirring once during cooking.

3. Stir in broth, apples, tomatoes and chutney. Cover; microwave on HIGH 7 minutes or until boiling, stirring once during cooking. Stir again.

4. Reduce power to 50%. Microwave 30 minutes or until meat is tender, stirring 3 times during cooking. Let stand, covered, 5 minutes.

5. Stir in sour cream. Garnish with peanuts; serve over rice. Makes about 5 cups or 6 servings.

Asparagus-Ham Roll-Ups

1 pound fresh asparagus
2 tablespoons water
8 slices (1 ounce each) boiled ham
**1 can (10¾ ounces) Campbell's Condensed Cream of
    Celery Soup**
½ cup sour cream
¼ cup milk
2 tablespoons chopped fresh parsley
1 teaspoon prepared mustard
Hot cooked rice

1. Arrange asparagus with tips toward center in 12- by 8-inch microwave-safe baking dish; add water. Cover with vented plastic wrap; microwave on HIGH 4 minutes or until asparagus is tender, rotating dish once during cooking. Drain well.

2. Divide asparagus spears among ham slices; roll ham around asparagus. Secure with wooden toothpicks if necessary. Arrange rolls in same baking dish.

3. In small bowl, stir soup until smooth; stir in sour cream, milk, parsley and mustard until well blended. Pour over ham rolls. Cover with vented plastic wrap; microwave at 50% power 13 minutes or until heated through. Let stand, covered, 5 minutes. Serve over rice. Makes 4 servings.

Note: Substitute 1 package (10 ounces) frozen asparagus spears for fresh asparagus. Cook frozen asparagus according to package directions. Drain well, then proceed as above in steps 2 and 3.

TIP   Reuse the plastic plates and domes from Le Menu Frozen Dinners and Entrées for storing and reheating your own leftover food. Refrigerate or freeze on plate, then cover with plastic dome and reheat in microwave oven at 50% power until warmed.

Pineapple-Glazed Ham and Sweets

Use leftover baked ham or ask for 1/4-inch-thick ham slices at the delicatessen.

1 can (8 ounces) pineapple slices in juice, undrained
1 package (12 ounces) Mrs. Paul's Frozen Candied Sweet
**   Potatoes**
1 tablespoon Dijon-style mustard
3/4 pound cooked ham, cut into 3 slices

1. Drain pineapple, reserving 2 tablespoons juice. To prepare sauce, in small bowl, stir together reserved pineapple juice, contents of sauce packet from sweet potatoes and mustard.

2. Arrange ham slices in center of 10-inch microwave-safe pie plate. Cut pineapple slices in half; arrange pineapple and sweet potatoes around edge of dish. Spoon sauce over.

3. Cover with vented plastic wrap; microwave on HIGH 10 minutes or until potatoes are tender, rotating dish once during cooking. Spoon sauce over ham and sweet potatoes before serving. Makes 3 servings.

Smothered Liver and Onions

2 tablespoons butter or margarine
1 large onion, thinly sliced
1 pound beef liver, 1/4 inch thick
1 can (10¾ ounces) Campbell's Condensed Cream of
**   Mushroom Soup**
1/4 cup milk or half-and-half
1/8 teaspoon pepper

1. In 12- by 8-inch microwave-safe baking dish, combine butter and onion. Cover with vented plastic wrap; microwave on HIGH 5 minutes or until onion is tender, stirring once during cooking.

2. Cut liver into 4 portions. Arrange liver over onions, placing thicker portions toward edges of dish. In small bowl, stir soup until smooth; stir in milk and pepper. Pour over liver. Cover; microwave on HIGH 10 minutes or until liver is no longer pink in center, rearranging liver twice during cooking. Let stand, covered, 5 minutes. Makes 4 servings.

PINEAPPLE-GLAZED HAM AND SWEETS ▶

Ham-Sauced Sweet Potatoes

3 sweet potatoes (about 8 ounces each)
**1 can (10¾ ounces) Campbell's Condensed Golden
    Mushroom Soup**
1 cup cooked ham cut into thin strips
½ teaspoon grated orange peel
⅓ cup orange juice
¼ cup raisins

1. Pierce potatoes with fork in several places; arrange in circular pattern on microwave-safe plate. Microwave, uncovered, on HIGH 8 minutes or until tender, rearranging potatoes once during cooking. Let stand, uncovered, while preparing sauce.

2. In medium microwave-safe bowl, combine remaining ingredients. Cover with vented plastic wrap; microwave on HIGH 4 minutes or until hot, stirring once during cooking. Split potatoes; spoon sauce over each. Makes 3 servings.

Ham and Dumplings

2 tablespoons butter or margarine
1 cup chopped zucchini
1 cup chopped carrots
1 clove garlic, minced
½ teaspoon dried basil leaves, crushed
⅛ teaspoon pepper
1 cup cubed cooked ham
**1 can (18¾ ounces) Campbell's Chunky Creamy Chicken
    with Mushrooms or Chunky Creamy Mushroom Soup**
1 cup biscuit mix
¼ cup milk
2 tablespoons chopped fresh parsley

1. In 2-quart microwave-safe casserole, combine butter, zucchini, carrots, garlic, basil and pepper. Cover with lid; microwave on HIGH 6 minutes or until vegetables are tender, stirring once during cooking.

2. Stir in ham and soup. Cover; microwave on HIGH 4 minutes or until hot and bubbling, stirring once during cooking.

3. Meanwhile, combine biscuit mix, milk and parsley until just blended. Drop by spoonfuls around edge of hot mixture to form 8 dumplings. Microwave, uncovered, on HIGH 4 minutes or until dumplings appear dry, rotating dish twice during cooking. Let stand, uncovered, 5 minutes. Makes 4 servings.

Warm Sausage and Potato Salad

Serve this hearty main dish on a bed of greens and call it a salad,
or serve it from the cooking dish and call it a casserole.

1 can (10½ ounces) Franco-American Chicken Gravy
4 green onions, sliced
2 tablespoons wine vinegar
1 tablespoon Dijon-style or grainy mustard
1½ pounds small potatoes, cut into ¼-inch slices
½ pound kielbasa or other smoked sausage, diced
2 tablespoons chopped fresh parsley

1. In 3-quart microwave-safe casserole, stir together gravy, onions, vinegar and mustard. Stir in potatoes and kielbasa.

2. Cover with lid; microwave on HIGH 25 minutes or until potatoes are tender, stirring twice during cooking. Let stand, covered, 5 minutes. Sprinkle with parsley. Makes about 5 cups or 4 servings.

Sausage and Potatoes Italiano

For a milder flavor, substitute 1 pound ground beef for the sausage.

1 pound hot Italian sausage, casing removed
½ cup chopped onion
4 cups thinly sliced potatoes
1¾ cups Prego al Fresco Spaghetti Sauce
¼ teaspoon pepper
1 cup shredded mozzarella cheese (4 ounces)

1. Crumble sausage into 2-quart microwave-safe casserole; stir in onion. Cover with lid; microwave on HIGH 5 minutes or until sausage is no longer pink, stirring once during cooking to break up meat. Spoon off fat.

2. Stir in potatoes, spaghetti sauce and pepper. Cover; microwave on HIGH 20 minutes or until potatoes are tender, stirring once during cooking. Sprinkle with cheese. Let stand, uncovered, 5 minutes. Makes 4 servings.

Sausage and Pepper Polenta

1 pound Italian sausage, casing removed
1 sweet red pepper, cut into strips
1 green pepper, cut into strips
1 large onion, thinly sliced
2 cloves garlic, minced
1 jar (15½ ounces) Prego Spaghetti Sauce
½ cup yellow cornmeal
1 teaspoon olive or vegetable oil
¼ teaspoon salt
2 cups water
⅓ cup grated Parmesan cheese

1. Crumble sausage into 8- by 8-inch microwave-safe baking dish. Add peppers, onion and garlic. Cover with vented plastic wrap; microwave on HIGH 10 minutes or until sausage is no longer pink, stirring twice during cooking to break up meat. Spoon off fat. Stir spaghetti sauce into sausage mixture; set aside.

2. In 2-quart microwave-safe casserole, combine cornmeal, oil and salt. Stir in water. Cover with lid; microwave on HIGH 8 minutes or until very thick, stirring 3 times during cooking.

3. Spread over sausage mixture. Cover with vented plastic wrap; microwave at 50% power 7 minutes or until very hot. Sprinkle with cheese. Let stand, covered, 10 minutes. Makes 6 servings.

Sausage Sandwiches: Omit last 5 ingredients. Prepare as above in step 1. Cover; microwave on HIGH 3 minutes or until hot and bubbling, stirring once during cooking. Spoon over 4 split hard rolls. Makes 4 sandwiches.

TIP   Summertime is one of the best reasons to own a microwave oven, because the kitchen will stay cool while you cook. Since microwave ovens heat only the food (unlike the range or conventional oven), the only heat that warms the air comes directly from the food.

Lasagna

½ pound Italian sausage, casing removed
1 cup chopped onion
1 jar (32 ounces) Prego Spaghetti Sauce
1 container (15 ounces) ricotta cheese
1 cup shredded mozzarella cheese (4 ounces)
2 eggs, beaten
9 lasagna noodles, cooked and drained
¼ cup grated Parmesan cheese

1. Crumble sausage into 2-quart microwave-safe casserole; stir in onion. Cover with lid; microwave on HIGH 5 minutes or until sausage is no longer pink, stirring once during cooking to break up meat. Spoon off fat.

2. Stir in spaghetti sauce. Cover; microwave on HIGH 5 minutes or until hot.

3. Meanwhile, in small bowl, stir together ricotta, mozzarella and eggs.

4. Spread 1 cup of the sauce mixture in 12- by 8-inch microwave-safe baking dish. Top with 3 lasagna noodles, ½ of the cheese mixture and 1 cup sauce. Repeat layers, ending with 3 noodles and remaining sauce.

5. Cover with vented plastic wrap; microwave at 50% power 30 to 35 minutes or until hot and bubbling, rotating dish twice during cooking. Sprinkle with Parmesan. Let stand, covered, 15 minutes. Makes 8 servings.

Bean and Kraut Franks

If you like franks with beans or sauerkraut, you're going to love this easy, hearty dish.

1 jar (16 ounces) Vlasic Old Fashioned Sauerkraut, rinsed and drained
1 can (16 ounces) Campbell's Pork & Beans in Tomato Sauce
1 small onion, chopped
2 tablespoons brown sugar
½ teaspoon caraway seeds
1 pound frankfurters or knockwurst

1. In 12- by 8-inch microwave-safe baking dish, stir together sauerkraut, pork and beans, onion, brown sugar and caraway. Cover with vented plastic wrap; microwave on HIGH 5 minutes or until hot, stirring once during cooking.

2. Arrange frankfurters over sauerkraut mixture. Cover; microwave on HIGH 5 minutes or until heated through, rotating dish once during cooking. Let stand, covered, 2 minutes. Makes 4 servings.

Eggs
and Cheese

Italian Mushroom Omelet

3 tablespoons butter or margarine
1 package (8 ounces) Campbell's Fresh Mushrooms,
    sliced (about 3 cups)
2 tablespoons chopped green pepper
1 jar (15½ ounces) Prego Spaghetti Sauce
2 tablespoons sliced pitted ripe olives
8 eggs
½ cup milk
⅛ teaspoon salt
½ cup shredded Cheddar cheese (2 ounces)

1. In 1½-quart microwave-safe casserole, combine 1 tablespoon of the butter, mushrooms and green pepper. Cover with lid; microwave on HIGH 3 minutes or until vegetables are tender, stirring once during cooking. Stir in spaghetti sauce and olives. Cover; microwave on HIGH 3 minutes or until hot and bubbling. Stir and set aside.

2. Place 1 tablespoon butter in 9-inch microwave-safe pie plate. Cover; microwave on HIGH 20 seconds or until melted. Brush onto pie plate.

3. In medium bowl, beat eggs, milk and salt until well blended. Pour ½ of the egg mixture into pie plate. Cover with waxed paper; microwave on HIGH 2 minutes. With spatula, gently move cooked outer edge of omelet to center, letting uncooked portion flow to edge. Cover; microwave on HIGH 2 minutes or until center is set. Remove omelet to serving plate.

4. Repeat steps 2 and 3 with remaining butter and egg mixture. Spoon about ½ cup sauce in center of each omelet; fold omelet in half. Top with more sauce and cheese. Serve with remaining sauce. Makes 4 servings.

ITALIAN MUSHROOM OMELET ▶

Apple-Cheddar Omelet

4 slices bacon, chopped
1 can (11 ounces) Campbell's Condensed Cheddar
   Cheese Soup/Sauce
8 eggs
⅓ cup milk
1 small apple, peeled and chopped
1 cup shredded Cheddar cheese (4 ounces)
⅛ teaspoon pepper

1. Place bacon in 9-inch microwave-safe pie plate. Cover with paper towel; microwave on HIGH 3 minutes or until crisp, stirring once during cooking. Remove bacon to paper towels; reserve bacon drippings in cup.

2. In medium bowl, stir ½ cup of the soup until smooth. Add eggs; beat until well blended. Set aside.

3. To make sauce: In 1-quart microwave-safe casserole, stir remaining soup until smooth; stir in milk, apple, cheese and pepper. Cover with lid; microwave on HIGH 4 minutes or until hot and bubbling, stirring once during cooking. Let stand, covered, while preparing omelets.

4. Brush 1 teaspoon of the bacon drippings over bottom and side of same pie plate. Pour in ½ of the egg mixture. Cover with waxed paper; microwave on HIGH 2 minutes. With spatula, gently move cooked outer edge of omelet to center, letting uncooked portion flow to edge. Cover; microwave on HIGH 2 minutes or until center is set. Fold omelet in half; slide onto serving plate.

5. Repeat step 4 with 1 teaspoon of the bacon drippings and remaining egg mixture. Spoon sauce over each omelet; sprinkle with bacon. Makes 4 servings.

Huevos Rancheros

  1 tablespoon vegetable oil
1/4 cup chopped green pepper
1/4 cup chopped onion
  2 teaspoons chili powder
  1 can (10¾ ounces) Campbell's Condensed Tomato Soup
1/4 cup water
  4 eggs
  4 corn tortillas (6-inch)
1/4 cup shredded Cheddar cheese (1 ounce)
    Chopped fresh parsley or cilantro for garnish

1. In 2-quart microwave-safe casserole, stir together oil, green pepper, onion and chili powder. Cover with lid; microwave on HIGH 3 minutes or until vegetables are tender, stirring once during cooking.

2. Stir in soup and water. Cover; microwave on HIGH 5 minutes or until edges are hot and bubbling, stirring once during cooking.

3. Gently break each egg, sliding onto soup mixture and arranging around edge of casserole. With toothpick, pierce each yolk. Cover; microwave at 50% power 4 minutes or until eggs are almost set, rotating dish once during cooking. Let stand, covered, 2 minutes.

4. Meanwhile, wrap stack of tortillas in damp paper towels. Microwave on HIGH 30 seconds or until warm.

5. Spoon 1 egg and some sauce onto each tortilla. Sprinkle 1 tablespoon cheese over each egg. Garnish with parsley. Makes 4 servings.

TIP Don't attempt to hard-cook eggs in the shell in the microwave oven; they will explode. For a quick substitution for chopped hard-cooked egg, simply scramble an egg in the microwave oven, then chop. To prepare, beat 1 egg until frothy in a small microwave-safe bowl. Cover with waxed paper; microwave on HIGH 1 minute or until egg is firm, stirring once during cooking. The fluffy texture is different from a hard-cooked egg, but works well in many dishes.

Campbelled Eggs

Nacho cheese soup brings a great new taste to this classic recipe.

1 can (about 11 ounces) Campbell's Condensed Nacho
    Cheese Soup/Dip, Cream of Chicken Soup or Cream
    of Mushroom Soup
8 eggs
    Chopped fresh parsley for garnish

1. In 3-quart microwave-safe casserole, stir soup until smooth. Add eggs; beat until smooth.

2. Cover with lid; microwave on HIGH 6½ minutes or until eggs are nearly set, stirring 3 times during cooking. Let stand, covered, 2 minutes. Garnish with parsley. Makes 4 servings.

Tortellini in Cream Sauce

1 teaspoon olive or vegetable oil
2 cloves garlic, minced
½ cup chopped sweet red pepper
¼ cup chopped onion
1 can (10¾ ounces) Campbell's Condensed Cream of
    Mushroom Soup
½ cup half-and-half or milk
¼ cup Chablis or other dry white wine
¼ teaspoon dried tarragon leaves, crushed
8 ounces cheese tortellini, cooked and drained
½ cup crumbled feta or grated Parmesan cheese
¼ cup sliced green onions

1. In 2-quart microwave-safe casserole, combine oil, garlic, red pepper and chopped onion. Cover with lid; microwave on HIGH 2 minutes or until vegetables are tender, stirring once during cooking.

2. Stir in soup until smooth. Stir in half-and-half, wine and tarragon. Cover; microwave on HIGH 5 minutes or until hot and bubbling, stirring once during cooking. Let stand, covered, 5 minutes.

3. Toss with hot tortellini. Sprinkle with cheese and green onions. Makes 4 servings.

Broccoli-Cheese Pie

**1 can (11 ounces) Campbell's Condensed Cheddar
   Cheese Soup/Sauce**
1½ cups cooked rice
4 eggs
**1 package (10 ounces) frozen chopped broccoli, cooked
   and drained**
1 cup ricotta cheese or creamed cottage cheese
1 sweet red pepper, cut into matchstick-thin strips
¼ teaspoon pepper

1. In medium bowl, stir ⅓ cup of the soup until smooth; stir in rice and 1 of the eggs. Press mixture onto bottom and side of 9-inch microwave-safe pie plate, forming a shell. Microwave, uncovered, on HIGH 2 minutes or until nearly set. Let stand, uncovered, while preparing filling.

2. In large bowl, stir remaining soup until smooth; stir in remaining 3 eggs, broccoli, ricotta, red pepper and pepper. Spoon into rice shell.

3. Microwave, uncovered, at 50% power 22 minutes or until center is set, rotating dish 3 times during cooking. Let stand, uncovered, 10 minutes. Makes 6 servings.

TIP   Frozen bagels and English muffins make better toast when they're thawed before toasting. Place frozen halves side by side on paper towels; microwave on HIGH 15 seconds.

Spinach-Tofu Lasagna

1 jar (15½ ounces) Prego Spaghetti Sauce
1 pound tofu, well drained
2 eggs
½ cup ricotta cheese
½ cup grated Parmesan cheese
1 package (10 ounces) frozen chopped spinach, thawed
    and well drained (see Note on page 54)
½ teaspoon Italian seasoning, crushed
⅛ teaspoon pepper
6 lasagna noodles, cooked and drained
2 cups shredded mozzarella cheese (8 ounces)

1. Heat spaghetti sauce according to label directions.

2. Meanwhile, in large bowl, mash tofu with fork. Stir in eggs, ricotta, ⅓ cup of the Parmesan, spinach, Italian seasoning and pepper until well mixed.

3. Spread 2 tablespoons of the spaghetti sauce in 8- by 8-inch microwave-safe baking dish. Fit 2 noodles into baking dish, cutting and piecing as needed. Layer ⅓ of the remaining sauce, ½ of the tofu mixture and ½ of the mozzarella over noodles. Repeat layers of 2 noodles, ⅓ of the sauce, remaining tofu mixture and remaining mozzarella. Top with remaining 2 noodles, remaining sauce and remaining Parmesan cheese.

4. Cover with vented plastic wrap; microwave on HIGH 8 minutes or until hot. Rotate dish. Reduce power to 50%. Microwave, covered, 12 minutes or until hot and bubbling, rotating dish twice during cooking. Let stand, covered, 5 minutes. Makes 6 servings.

TIP To avoid washing another dish, microwave Prego Spaghetti Sauce according to label directions in a large microwave-safe bowl covered with vented plastic wrap. Add hot pasta, toss and serve directly from the bowl.

Eggplant Parmesan

This microwave method helps you avoid extra calories. Most conventional eggplant recipes require oil for frying or broiling, but you don't need any here.

1 egg
2 tablespoons milk
1 cup Italian-seasoned fine dry bread crumbs
1 medium eggplant, peeled and cut into ¼-inch slices
    (1 pound)
1 jar (15½ ounces) Prego Spaghetti Sauce
2 cups shredded mozzarella cheese (8 ounces)
2 tablespoons grated Parmesan cheese

1. In pie plate, beat together egg and milk. Place bread crumbs in another pie plate. Dip eggplant slices in egg mixture, then in crumbs to coat well.

2. Arrange ½ of the eggplant slices on a 10-inch microwave-safe plate lined with paper towels. Microwave, uncovered, on HIGH 4 minutes or until tender, rearranging slices once during cooking. Repeat with remaining eggplant.

3. Spread ¼ cup of the spaghetti sauce in 8- by 8-inch microwave-safe baking dish. Layer ½ of the eggplant, ½ of the mozzarella and ½ of the remaining spaghetti sauce in dish; repeat layers. Sprinkle with Parmesan cheese.

4. Cover with vented plastic wrap; microwave on HIGH 4 minutes or until hot. Rotate dish. Reduce power to 50%. Microwave, covered, 10 minutes or until hot and bubbling, rotating dish once during cooking. Let stand, covered, 5 minutes. Makes 4 servings.

Side Dishes

Marinated Vegetables

Here's a great way to put lots of flavor into your vegetables with very few added calories. It's wonderful for parties, too, because everything is done in advance and the vegetables marinate until you're ready to serve them.

    1 cup carrots cut into matchstick-thin strips
½ pound green beans, cut into 1-inch lengths
    2 tablespoons finely chopped onion
    1 large sweet red pepper, cut into matchstick-thin strips
    1 large zucchini, cut into matchstick-thin strips
1½ cups "V8" Vegetable Juice
    2 tablespoons vinegar
    1 tablespoon vegetable oil
    1 teaspoon chili powder
    Salad greens

1. In 12- by 8-inch microwave-safe baking dish, combine carrots, beans and onion. Cover with vented plastic wrap; microwave on HIGH 4 minutes or until vegetables are nearly tender, stirring once during cooking.

2. Stir in pepper and zucchini. Cover; microwave on HIGH 4 minutes or until vegetables are tender-crisp, stirring once during cooking.

3. In small bowl, stir together "V8" juice, vinegar, oil and chili powder. Pour over warm vegetables. Cover; refrigerate until serving time, at least 4 hours. Serve on salad greens. Makes about 5 cups or 8 servings.

Note: Substitute 1 package (9 ounces) frozen cut green beans for fresh beans.

MARINATED VEGETABLES ▶

Green Bean Casserole

2 packages (9 ounces each) frozen cut green beans
1 can (10¾ ounces) Campbell's Condensed Cream of
    Mushroom Soup
½ cup milk
1 teaspoon soy sauce
    Dash pepper
½ cup sliced pitted ripe olives (optional)
1 can (2.8 ounces) French-fried onions

1. Place beans in medium microwave-safe bowl. Cover with vented plastic wrap; microwave on HIGH 9 minutes or until tender, stirring twice during cooking. Drain.

2. In 1½-quart microwave-safe casserole, stir soup until smooth. Add milk, soy sauce and pepper; stir until well blended. Stir in beans, ½ of the olives and ½ of the onions. Cover with lid; microwave on HIGH 7 minutes or until hot and bubbling, stirring once during cooking. Let stand, covered, 5 minutes. Sprinkle with remaining olives and onions. Makes 6 servings.

Note: Substitute 4 cups (about 1 pound) fresh cut green beans and 2 tablespoons water for the frozen green beans.

Beans Italiano

1 tablespoon olive or vegetable oil
1 clove garlic, minced
¼ teaspoon dried oregano leaves, crushed
1 can (16 ounces) Campbell's Pork & Beans in Tomato
    Sauce
1 can (8 ounces) whole tomatoes, undrained, cut up
1 can (8 ounces) cut green beans, drained
1 cup cooked small shell pasta (½ cup uncooked)

1. In 2-quart microwave-safe casserole, combine oil, garlic and oregano. Cover with lid; microwave on HIGH 1 minute.

2. Stir in pork and beans, tomatoes with their liquid, green beans and pasta. Cover; microwave on HIGH 5 minutes or until hot and bubbling, stirring once during cooking. Makes about 4 cups or 6 servings.

Cauliflower in Cheese Sauce

1 medium head cauliflower (about 2 pounds)
2 tablespoons water
1 can (10¾ ounces) Campbell's Condensed Cream of
    Mushroom Soup
1 cup shredded Cheddar cheese (4 ounces)
½ cup milk
    Dash ground nutmeg
    Dash pepper
    Toasted sliced almonds for garnish

1. Remove and discard core and outside leaves of cauliflower. Place whole cauliflower in 2-quart microwave-safe casserole; add water. Cover with lid; microwave on HIGH 10 minutes or until tender, rotating dish once during cooking. Let stand, covered, while preparing sauce.

2. In medium microwave-safe bowl, stir soup until smooth. Add cheese, milk, nutmeg and pepper; stir until well blended. Cover with vented plastic wrap; microwave on HIGH 5 minutes or until hot and bubbling, stirring once during cooking.

3. Place cauliflower on platter; spoon ½ of the sauce over cauliflower. Garnish with almonds. Serve with remaining sauce. Makes 8 servings.

Note: To toast almonds: In small microwave-safe bowl, combine ¼ cup sliced or chopped almonds and 1 teaspoon butter or margarine. Microwave, uncovered, on HIGH 1½ minutes or until almonds begin to brown, stirring once during cooking.

TIP If you have trouble cutting through hard vegetables such as winter squash, pierce in several places, then microwave the whole vegetable on HIGH about 1 minute to soften it slightly.

Broccoli and Celery Oriental

1 tablespoon vegetable oil
3 cups broccoli flowerets
1½ cups thinly sliced celery
¼ cup sliced green onions
2 tablespoons chopped pimento
1 can (10½ ounces) Franco-American Chicken Gravy
1 tablespoon soy sauce
   Cashews for garnish

1. In 2-quart microwave-safe casserole, combine oil, broccoli, celery and green onions. Cover with lid; microwave on HIGH 4 minutes or until vegetables are tender-crisp, stirring once during cooking.

2. Stir in pimento, gravy and soy sauce. Cover; microwave on HIGH 3 minutes or until hot and bubbling. Garnish with cashews. Makes about 3 cups or 4 servings.

Broccoli and Cauliflower Medley

1 package (10 ounces) frozen broccoli spears
1 package (10 ounces) frozen cauliflower
1 can (10¾ ounces) Campbell's Condensed Cream of
   Mushroom Soup
⅓ cup milk
½ cup coarsely crushed Pepperidge Farm Onion and
   Garlic Croutons

1. In 2-quart microwave-safe casserole, combine broccoli and cauliflower. Cover with lid; microwave on HIGH 8 minutes or until vegetables are thawed, stirring once during cooking. Drain. Cut broccoli into bite-size pieces.

2. In small bowl, stir soup until smooth; stir in milk. Pour over vegetables. Cover; microwave on HIGH 8 minutes or until hot and bubbling, stirring twice during cooking. Let stand, covered, 3 minutes. Sprinkle with croutons. Makes about 4 cups or 6 servings.

BROCCOLI AND CELERY ORIENTAL ▶

Copper Pennies

2 pounds carrots, thinly sliced
¼ cup water
1 can (10¾ ounces) Campbell's Condensed Tomato Soup
½ cup vinegar
¼ cup vegetable oil
¼ cup sugar
1 teaspoon dry mustard
1 teaspoon Worcestershire sauce
1 cup thinly sliced celery
1 medium onion, thinly sliced

1. In 3-quart microwave-safe casserole, combine carrots and water. Cover with lid; microwave on HIGH 10 minutes or until carrots are tender-crisp, stirring twice during cooking. Drain.

2. In large bowl, stir together soup, vinegar, oil, sugar, mustard and Worcestershire. Stir in carrots, celery and onion. Cover; refrigerate until serving time, at least 4 hours. Makes about 7 cups or 12 servings.

Dilled Carrots and Parsnips

1 can (10¾ ounces) Campbell's Condensed Cream of
    Celery Soup
½ cup milk
¼ teaspoon dried dill weed, crushed
2 cups carrots cut into 1-inch-long sticks
2 cups parsnips cut into 1-inch-long sticks

1. In 3-quart microwave-safe casserole, stir soup until smooth. Add milk and dill weed; stir until well blended. Stir in carrots. Cover with lid; microwave on HIGH 6 minutes.

2. Stir in parsnips. Cover; microwave on HIGH 13 minutes or until vegetables are nearly tender, stirring twice during cooking. Let stand, covered, 5 minutes. Makes 6 servings.

Dilled Carrots: Prepare as above but use 4 cups carrots and omit parsnips. Microwave a total of 19 minutes, stirring twice during cooking.

Nutty Spinach Casserole

This special side dish is a good choice for a party menu, yet it's easy enough to serve on a busy weeknight, too.

2 packages (10 ounces each) frozen chopped spinach
1 can (10¾ ounces) Campbell's Condensed Cream of Mushroom Soup
2 eggs
½ cup shredded Monterey Jack cheese (2 ounces)
¼ cup chopped green onions
¼ cup chopped walnuts, toasted
2 tablespoons grated Parmesan cheese

1. Place spinach in 1½-quart microwave-safe casserole. Cover with lid; microwave on HIGH 8 minutes or until spinach is heated through, stirring twice during cooking. Drain well.

2. Stir in soup until smooth; stir in remaining ingredients until well blended. Microwave, uncovered, on HIGH 12 minutes or until set in center, rotating dish twice during cooking. Makes 6 servings.

Note: To toast walnuts: In small microwave-safe bowl, combine ¼ cup chopped walnuts and 1 teaspoon butter or margarine. Microwave, uncovered, on HIGH 2 minutes or until walnuts begin to brown, stirring twice during cooking.

Okra Creole

1 tablespoon vegetable oil
1 cup sliced celery
1 large green pepper, cut into strips
½ cup chopped onion
1 bay leaf
¼ teaspoon dried thyme leaves, crushed
⅛ teaspoon ground red pepper (cayenne)
1 package (10 ounces) frozen sliced okra, cooked and drained
1 can (10¾ ounces) Campbell's Condensed Tomato Soup

1. In 2-quart microwave-safe casserole, combine oil, celery, green pepper, onion, bay leaf, thyme and red pepper. Cover with lid; microwave on HIGH 5 minutes or until vegetables are tender, stirring once during cooking.

2. Stir in okra and soup. Cover; microwave on HIGH 3 minutes or until hot and bubbling. Remove bay leaf. Makes about 4 cups or 6 servings.

Fresh Vegetable Ring

This recipe demonstrates how the arrangement of food can compensate for differences in cooking time. Dense vegetables, such as broccoli and cauliflower, which take longer to cook than soft vegetables, are placed around the edge of the platter where they absorb more microwave energy.

2 cups broccoli flowerets
2 cups cauliflowerets
1 small zucchini, cut into ¼-inch slices
1 small yellow squash, cut into ¼-inch slices
1 can (10¾ ounces) Campbell's Condensed Chicken Broth
6 medium Campbell's Fresh Mushrooms, halved
Sweet red pepper strips for garnish
2 teaspoons cornstarch
1 teaspoon chopped fresh basil leaves or ½ teaspoon dried basil leaves, crushed
1 teaspoon wine vinegar

1. Arrange broccoli in a circle around rim of a 12-inch round microwave-safe platter. Arrange cauliflower next to broccoli. Arrange alternate slices of zucchini and yellow squash next to cauliflower, leaving space in center of platter. Pour ¼ cup of the broth over vegetables. Cover with vented plastic wrap; microwave on HIGH 5 minutes, rotating dish once during cooking.

2. Place mushrooms in center of platter. Garnish with red pepper strips. Cover; microwave on HIGH 2 minutes or until vegetables are tender-crisp. Let stand, covered, while preparing sauce.

3. In small microwave-safe bowl, blend remaining broth, cornstarch, basil and vinegar until smooth. Cover with vented plastic wrap; microwave on HIGH 2 minutes or until mixture boils, stirring twice during cooking. Spoon over vegetables. Makes 6 servings.

FRESH VEGETABLE RING ▶

Ratatouille

   2 tablespoons olive or vegetable oil
   ½ cup coarsely chopped onion
   1 medium sweet red pepper, cut into 1-inch squares
   2 cloves garlic, minced
   1 can (11 ounces) Campbell's Condensed Zesty Tomato
      Soup/Sauce
   1 small eggplant, peeled and cut into 1-inch cubes (about
      4 cups)
   2 medium zucchini, cut into ¼-inch slices (about
      4 cups)
   1 cup sliced pitted ripe olives

1. In 3-quart microwave-safe casserole, combine oil, onion, red pepper and garlic. Cover with lid; microwave on HIGH 4 minutes or until vegetables are tender, stirring once during cooking.

2. Add soup, eggplant, zucchini and olives; stir to mix well. Cover; microwave on HIGH 15 minutes or until vegetables are tender, stirring twice during cooking. Let stand, covered, 5 minutes. Makes about 6 cups or 8 servings.

Onions in Herb Sauce

   6 medium onions (about 1½ pounds), peeled
   1 can (11 ounces) Campbell's Condensed Cheddar
      Cheese Soup/Sauce
   2 tablespoons wine vinegar
   2 tablespoons chopped fresh dill weed or 2 teaspoons
      dried dill weed, crushed
   1 tablespoon Dijon-style mustard
   ½ cup sour cream

1. Cut ½-inch-deep "X" in top of each onion. Place in 2-quart microwave-safe casserole; set aside.

2. In small bowl, stir soup until smooth. Stir in vinegar, dill and mustard. Pour over onions. Cover with lid; microwave on HIGH 12 minutes or until onions are fork-tender, rotating dish once during cooking. Let stand, covered, 5 minutes.

3. Remove onions to serving plate. Stir sour cream into sauce until smooth. Spoon some sauce over onions; pass remainder. Makes 6 servings.

Spaghetti Squash Primavera

1 small spaghetti squash (about 2 pounds)
1 tablespoon olive or vegetable oil
1 medium sweet red pepper, cut into matchstick-thin
    strips
1 medium zucchini, cut into matchstick-thin strips
1 clove garlic, minced
1 can (10½ ounces) Campbell's Chunky Creamy
    Mushroom Soup
⅓ cup grated Parmesan cheese

1. Pierce spaghetti squash several times with fork. Place squash on microwave-safe plate. Microwave, uncovered, on HIGH 12 minutes or until fork-tender, turning over once during cooking. Let stand while preparing sauce.

2. In 2-quart microwave-safe casserole, combine oil, red pepper, zucchini and garlic. Cover with lid; microwave on HIGH 3 minutes or until vegetables are tender, stirring once during cooking.

3. Stir soup and cheese into vegetable mixture. Cover; microwave on HIGH 3 minutes or until hot and bubbling.

4. Halve squash lengthwise; remove seeds. With fork, lift out spaghetti-like strands to serving platter; discard squash shells. Pour sauce over squash. Serve with additional Parmesan cheese. Makes 4 servings.

Zucchini Marinara

1 pound zucchini, cut into ¼-inch slices (about 4 cups)
1 cup Prego al Fresco Spaghetti Sauce
2 tablespoons chopped fresh parsley
2 tablespoons chopped fresh basil leaves or 1 teaspoon
    dried basil leaves, crushed
1 tablespoon lemon juice
¼ cup grated Parmesan cheese

1. In 2-quart microwave-safe casserole, combine zucchini, spaghetti sauce, parsley, basil and lemon juice. Cover with lid; microwave on HIGH 8 minutes or until zucchini is nearly tender, stirring twice during cooking.

2. Stir in Parmesan cheese. Let stand, covered, 5 minutes. Makes about 4 cups or 6 servings.

Vegetables in Cheese Sauce

    1 can (11 ounces) Campbell's Condensed Cheddar
        Cheese Soup/Sauce
    1/3 cup milk
    1/2 teaspoon dried basil leaves, crushed
    1 clove garlic, minced
    2 cups cauliflowerets
    1 small onion, cut into thin wedges
    1 1/2 cups diagonally sliced carrots
    1 package (10 ounces) frozen peas

1. In 3-quart microwave-safe casserole, stir soup until smooth. Stir in milk, basil and garlic; mix well.

2. Add vegetables; stir to coat well. Cover with lid; microwave on HIGH 15 minutes or until vegetables are tender, stirring twice during cooking. Let stand, covered, 5 minutes. Makes about 5 1/2 cups or 8 servings.

Saucy Sweet Potatoes

    3 slices bacon, chopped
    1 package (20 ounces) Mrs. Paul's Frozen Candied Sweet
        Potatoes
    1 can (8 ounces) sliced water chestnuts, drained
    1/2 teaspoon grated orange peel
    1/3 cup orange juice

1. Place bacon in 2-quart microwave-safe casserole. Cover with paper towel; microwave on HIGH 3 minutes or until crisp, stirring once during cooking. Remove bacon to paper towels, reserving drippings in casserole.

2. Stir contents of sauce packet from sweet potatoes into drippings until smooth. Stir in sweet potatoes, water chestnuts, orange peel and juice. Cover with lid; microwave on HIGH 9 minutes or until potatoes are tender, stirring once during cooking. Let stand, covered, 5 minutes. Sprinkle bacon over potatoes. Makes 5 servings.

VEGETABLES IN CHEESE SAUCE ▶

Chili Potatoes

1 can (11¼ ounces) Campbell's Condensed Chili Beef
   Soup
¼ cup water
¼ teaspoon ground cumin
3 cups thinly sliced potatoes
½ cup chopped onion
1 cup shredded Monterey Jack cheese with jalapeño
   peppers (4 ounces)

1. In 2-quart microwave-safe casserole, stir together soup, water and cumin until smooth.

2. Stir in potatoes and onion. Cover with lid; microwave on HIGH 18 minutes or until potatoes are tender, stirring twice during cooking. Top with cheese. Let stand, covered, 5 minutes. Makes 6 servings.

Lyonnaise Potatoes

Here's a dish to delight those who love potatoes and gravy; the potatoes cook right in the gravy, absorbing all its savory goodness.

3 cups thinly sliced onions
1 clove garlic, minced
1 can (10½ ounces) Franco-American Chicken Gravy
4 cups thinly sliced potatoes
⅛ teaspoon pepper
½ teaspoon paprika

1. In 12- by 8-inch microwave-safe baking dish, stir together onions, garlic and gravy. Cover with vented plastic wrap; microwave on HIGH 5 minutes or until onions are tender, stirring once during cooking.

2. Stir in potatoes and pepper; sprinkle with paprika. Cover; microwave on HIGH 18 minutes or until potatoes are tender, rotating dish twice during cooking. Let stand, covered, 5 minutes. Makes 6 servings.

Potato and Cheese Casserole

If desired, you can leave the peels on the potatoes for a more homey casserole.

**1 can (10¾ ounces) Campbell's Condensed Cream of
    Celery Soup**
1 cup shredded Cheddar cheese (4 ounces)
½ cup milk
  Generous dash pepper
1 large clove garlic, minced
4 cups thinly sliced potatoes
1 cup thinly sliced onions

1. In medium bowl, stir soup until smooth. Add cheese, milk, pepper and garlic; stir until well blended.

2. In 2-quart microwave-safe casserole, layer ½ of the potatoes, ½ of the onions and ½ of the soup mixture. Repeat layers.

3. Cover with lid; microwave on HIGH 23 minutes or until potatoes are tender, rotating dish 3 times during cooking. Let stand, covered, 5 minutes. Makes 6 servings.

TIP   Do you miss the crunch of a browned topping on a casserole or vegetable dish? Add one of these just before serving to improve appearance, flavor and texture: crushed potato or corn chips, canned French-fried onions, croutons (whole or crushed), toasted slivered almonds or chopped peanuts, crushed cornflakes or other cereal or crushed crackers (your favorite variety).

Creamy Cabbage

1 medium head cabbage, shredded (about 8 cups)
1 can (10¾ ounces) Campbell's Condensed Creamy
    Onion Soup/Dip
⅓ cup milk
1 tablespoon vinegar
1 teaspoon caraway seeds
¼ cup grated Parmesan cheese
    Green pepper rings for garnish

1. Place cabbage in 3-quart microwave-safe casserole. In small bowl, stir soup until smooth; stir in milk, vinegar and caraway until blended. Pour over cabbage. Cover with lid; microwave on HIGH 15 minutes or until cabbage is tender, stirring twice during cooking.

2. Stir in Parmesan. Let stand, covered, 5 minutes. Garnish with green pepper rings. Makes about 5 cups or 8 servings.

Corn Pudding

1 can (10¾ ounces) Campbell's Condensed Cream of
    Celery Soup
1 cup milk
⅓ cup yellow cornmeal
¼ cup butter or margarine
4 eggs, beaten
1 can (about 16 ounces) whole kernel golden corn,
    drained
½ cup chopped sweet red pepper
½ teaspoon hot pepper sauce

1. In 3-quart microwave-safe casserole, stir soup until smooth. Add milk and cornmeal; stir until well blended. Cover with lid; microwave on HIGH 6 minutes or until boiling, stirring twice during cooking. Stir in butter. Let stand, covered, 5 minutes.

2. In medium bowl, combine eggs, corn, pepper and hot pepper sauce. Gradually stir egg mixture into soup mixture until well blended. Cover; microwave on HIGH 6 minutes, stirring once during cooking. Stir again.

3. Reduce power to 50%. Cover; microwave 12 minutes or until knife inserted near center comes out clean, rotating dish twice during cooking. Let stand, covered, 5 minutes. Makes 6 servings.

CREAMY CABBAGE ▶

Mushroom Risotto

1 tablespoon butter or margarine
½ cup finely chopped onion
1 can (10¾ ounces) Campbell's Condensed Chicken
   Broth
½ cup water
¼ cup Chablis or other dry white wine
1 cup regular long-grain rice, uncooked
1 cup sliced Campbell's Fresh Mushrooms
½ cup grated Parmesan cheese
   Chopped fresh parsley for garnish

1. In 2-quart microwave-safe casserole, combine butter and onion. Cover with lid; microwave on HIGH 3 minutes or until onion is tender, stirring once during cooking.

2. Stir in broth, water and wine. Cover; microwave on HIGH 2 minutes or until hot.

3. Stir in rice. Cover; microwave on HIGH 10 minutes or until bubbling. Stir in mushrooms. Cover; microwave at 50% power 10 minutes or until rice is nearly done. Stir in cheese. Let stand, covered, 5 minutes. Garnish with parsley. Makes about 3 cups or 6 servings.

Spanish Rice and Beans

1 can (11¼ ounces) Campbell's Condensed Chili Beef
   Soup
1½ cups "V8" Vegetable Juice
1 cup quick-cooking rice, uncooked
½ cup water
½ cup chopped green pepper or 1 can (4 ounces) chopped
   green chilies, drained

In 1½-quart microwave-safe casserole, stir together all ingredients until well blended. Cover with lid; microwave on HIGH 10 minutes or until rice is done, stirring once during cooking. Let stand, covered, 5 minutes. Stir before serving. Makes about 3½ cups or 6 servings.

TIP   Each 8-ounce package of Campbell's Fresh Mushrooms contains enough for about 3 cups sliced or 2½ cups chopped mushrooms.

Louisiana Beans and Rice

Serve this as a side dish or in larger servings as a main dish.

1 tablespoon vegetable oil
1 cup chopped onion
1 large green pepper, chopped
2 cloves garlic, minced
½ teaspoon dried thyme leaves, crushed
¼ teaspoon dried oregano leaves, crushed
2 cans (16 ounces each) red beans or pinto beans,
   drained
1 can (10¾ ounces) Campbell's Condensed Tomato Soup
1 cup diced cooked ham or smoked sausage
¼ teaspoon ground red pepper (cayenne)
   Hot cooked rice

1. In 2-quart microwave-safe casserole, combine oil, onion, green pepper, garlic, thyme and oregano. Cover with lid; microwave on HIGH 5 minutes or until vegetables are tender, stirring once during cooking.

2. Stir in beans, soup, ham and red pepper. Cover; microwave on HIGH 5 minutes or until hot. Stir.

3. Reduce power to 50%. Cover; microwave 15 minutes or until flavors are blended. Serve over rice. Makes about 5 cups or 5 servings.

Rice Olé

1 can (10¾ ounces) Campbell's Condensed Cream of
   Celery Soup
1 cup plain yogurt
1 can (4 ounces) chopped green chilies, drained
¼ cup chopped onion
4 cups cooked rice (1⅓ cups uncooked)
1½ cups shredded Monterey Jack cheese (6 ounces)
¼ cup grated Parmesan cheese
   Paprika for garnish

1. In large bowl, stir soup until smooth. Add yogurt, chilies and onion; stir until well blended. Stir in rice and Monterey Jack cheese.

2. Spread mixture evenly in 12- by 8-inch microwave-safe baking dish. Cover with waxed paper; microwave on HIGH 9 minutes or until edges are bubbling and center is hot, rotating dish once during cooking.

3. Sprinkle with Parmesan and paprika. Microwave, uncovered, 1 minute. Let stand 5 minutes. Makes 8 servings.

Pasta with Vegetables

   1 teaspoon olive or vegetable oil
   2 medium zucchini, cut into 1½-inch-long sticks
   1 sweet red pepper, cut into ½-inch squares
  ½ cup chopped onion
   2 cloves garlic, minced
   1 can (11 ounces) Campbell's Condensed Zesty Tomato
      Soup/Sauce
  ½ cup water
  ¼ cup Chablis or other dry white wine
   8 ounces thin spaghetti or other pasta, cooked and
      drained
    Grated Parmesan cheese for garnish

1. In 2-quart microwave-safe casserole, combine oil, zucchini, red pepper, onion and garlic. Cover with lid; microwave on HIGH 4 minutes or until vegetables are tender, stirring once during cooking.

2. Stir in soup, water and wine. Cover; microwave on HIGH 7 minutes or until hot and bubbling, stirring once during cooking. Let stand, covered, 5 minutes. Serve over hot pasta. Garnish with Parmesan cheese. Makes 8 servings.

Saffron Rice

   1 tablespoon olive or vegetable oil
   2 cloves garlic, minced
   1 cup regular long-grain rice, uncooked
   1 can (14½ ounces) Swanson Clear Ready to Serve
      Chicken Broth
  ¼ cup water
  ⅛ teaspoon saffron, crushed, or generous dash turmeric
  ½ cup sliced green onions
  ¼ cup toasted sliced almonds (see Note on page 125)

1. In 2-quart microwave-safe casserole, combine oil and garlic. Cover with lid; microwave on HIGH 1 minute.

2. Stir in rice, broth, water and saffron. Cover; microwave on HIGH 10 minutes. Stir.

3. Reduce power to 50%. Cover; microwave 10 minutes or until rice is nearly done. Stir in green onions and almonds. Let stand, covered, 5 minutes or until rice is tender. Makes about 3½ cups or 5 servings.

PASTA WITH VEGETABLES ▶

Spinach and Noodles Parmesan

     ½ cup chopped onion
      1 package (10 ounces) frozen chopped spinach
      1 can (10¾ ounces) Campbell's Condensed Cream of
           Celery Soup
     ½ cup sour cream
     ½ cup grated Parmesan cheese
     ⅛ teaspoon black pepper
     ⅛ teaspoon ground nutmeg
          Generous dash ground red pepper (cayenne)
      2 cups cooked wide egg noodles (6 ounces uncooked)

1. Place onion in 2-quart microwave-safe casserole. Cover with lid; microwave on HIGH 3 minutes or until tender, stirring once during cooking.

2. Add spinach. Cover; microwave on HIGH 5 minutes or until spinach is thawed, stirring twice during cooking. Stir in soup; stir in sour cream, cheese, black pepper, nutmeg and red pepper.

3. Cover; microwave at 50% power 8 minutes or until hot, stirring once during cooking. Add hot noodles; toss to coat. Makes about 5 cups or 8 servings.

Garden Macaroni and Cheese

      2 packages (10 ounces each) Swanson Frozen Homestyle
           Macaroni and Cheese
     ¼ cup chopped green onions
     ½ teaspoon dried basil leaves, crushed
      1 cup chopped tomato
     ¼ cup sliced pitted ripe olives

1. In 2-quart microwave-safe casserole, combine frozen macaroni and cheese, onions and basil. Cover with lid; microwave on HIGH 10 minutes or until warm, stirring twice during cooking.

2. Stir in tomato and olives. Cover; microwave on HIGH 3 minutes or until hot and bubbling. Makes about 4 cups or 4 servings.

Note: To halve this recipe, use only half the amount of each ingredient and cook in 1½-quart microwave-safe casserole. In step 1, microwave on HIGH 5 minutes, stirring once during cooking; in step 2, microwave on HIGH 2 minutes.

SPINACH AND NOODLES PARMESAN ▶

Mexicali Vegetables and Pasta

*Add crunch to this festive dish by sprinkling with crushed corn chips
just before serving.*

> **2 tablespoons butter or margarine**
> **2 cups chopped zucchini**
> **$1/2$ cup thinly sliced celery**
> **$1/4$ cup chopped onion**
> **$1/4$ teaspoon dried oregano leaves, crushed**
> **1 can (11 ounces) Campbell's Condensed Nacho Cheese
>   Soup/Dip**
> **$1/3$ cup milk**
> **2 cups cooked corkscrew macaroni (1 cup uncooked)**
> **2 medium tomatoes, chopped**

1. In 3-quart microwave-safe casserole, combine butter, zucchini, celery, onion and oregano. Cover with lid; microwave on HIGH 5 minutes or until vegetables are tender, stirring once during cooking.

2. In small bowl, stir soup until smooth; stir in milk. Add soup mixture, pasta and tomatoes to vegetables. Cover; microwave on HIGH 5 minutes or until hot and bubbling, stirring once during cooking. Let stand, covered, 5 minutes. Makes about 4 cups or 4 servings.

TIP   Don't sprinkle salt over vegetables or other foods before microwaving. The salt attracts microwave energy and can cause overcooking in spots. Instead, add salt to cooking liquid or salt foods after cooking.

Double Celery Stuffing

2 tablespoons butter or margarine
1½ cups chopped celery
½ cup chopped onion
1 teaspoon rubbed sage
1 can (10¾ ounces) Campbell's Condensed Cream of Celery Soup
½ cup shredded carrot
5 cups cubed stale bread

1. In 2-quart microwave-safe casserole, combine butter, celery, onion and sage. Cover with lid; microwave on HIGH 5 minutes or until vegetables are tender-crisp, stirring once during cooking.

2. Stir in soup until smooth. Stir in carrot and bread cubes. Microwave, uncovered, on HIGH 8 minutes or until heated through, stirring twice during cooking. Makes 5 cups or 8 servings.

Note: If your bread isn't stale, arrange 8 slices fresh bread in a single layer on paper towel in microwave oven. Microwave, uncovered, on HIGH 3 minutes, rearranging bread slices once during cooking. Let stand, uncovered, on wire rack 10 minutes.

Corn Bread Stuffing

½ pound bulk pork sausage
1 cup chopped onion
½ cup chopped celery
¼ cup butter or margarine
2 large apples, chopped
1 cup Swanson Clear Ready to Serve Chicken Broth
1 package (8 ounces) Pepperidge Farm Corn Bread Stuffing Mix
¼ cup chopped pecans
¼ cup chopped fresh parsley

1. Crumble sausage into 3-quart microwave-safe casserole; stir in onion and celery. Cover with lid; microwave on HIGH 5 minutes or until sausage is no longer pink, stirring once during cooking to break up meat.

2. Stir in butter, apples and broth. Cover; microwave on HIGH 5 minutes or until apples are tender and broth is boiling, stirring once during cooking.

3. Stir in stuffing mix, pecans and parsley. Let stand, covered, 5 minutes. Makes about 6½ cups or 10 servings.

Tangy Bulgur Salad

1 can (10¾ ounces) Campbell's Condensed Chicken
    Broth
¾ cup bulgur wheat, uncooked
½ cup chopped fresh parsley
1 medium tomato, seeded and chopped
¼ cup lemon juice
¼ cup olive or vegetable oil
1 tablespoon chopped fresh mint leaves or 1 teaspoon
    dried mint leaves, crushed (optional)
¼ teaspoon pepper
    Lettuce leaves (optional)
    Sliced tomatoes (optional)

1. In 1½-quart microwave-safe casserole, stir together broth and bulgur. Cover with lid; microwave on HIGH 6 minutes or until liquid is absorbed and bulgur is tender, stirring once during cooking.

2. Stir in parsley, chopped tomato, lemon juice, oil, mint and pepper. Cover; refrigerate until serving time, at least 4 hours.

3. Line serving plate with lettuce and tomato slices. Spoon bulgur mixture over tomato slices. Garnish with additional fresh mint leaves. Makes about 3½ cups or 6 servings.

Warm Bean Salad

1 tablespoon vegetable oil
¾ cup chopped celery
2 green onions, thinly sliced
1 can (16 ounces) Campbell's Home Style Beans
1 tablespoon chopped fresh parsley
1 tablespoon red wine vinegar
⅛ teaspoon pepper
1 tomato, chopped

1. In 1½-quart microwave-safe casserole, combine oil, celery and onions. Cover with lid; microwave on HIGH 1½ minutes or until celery is tender-crisp.

2. Stir in beans, parsley, vinegar and pepper. Cover; microwave on HIGH 2½ minutes or until heated through, stirring once during cooking. Stir in tomato. Makes about 3 cups or 4 servings.

TANGY BULGUR SALAD ▶

German Potato Salad

6 medium potatoes (2 pounds)
6 slices bacon, chopped
½ cup chopped onion
½ cup sliced celery
2 tablespoons all-purpose flour
1 can (10¾ ounces) Campbell's Condensed Chicken Broth
¼ cup vinegar
2 tablespoons sugar
⅛ teaspoon pepper
2 tablespoons chopped fresh parsley

1. Pierce potatoes with fork in several places; arrange in circular pattern on microwave-safe plate. Microwave, uncovered, on HIGH 10 minutes or until tender, rearranging potatoes once during cooking. Let stand while preparing sauce.

2. Place bacon in 3-quart microwave-safe casserole. Cover with paper towel; microwave on HIGH 4 minutes or until crisp, stirring once during cooking. Remove to paper towels, reserving drippings in casserole.

3. Stir onion and celery into bacon drippings. Cover with lid; microwave on HIGH 3 minutes or until vegetables are tender-crisp, stirring once during cooking.

4. Stir in flour until smooth. Gradually stir in broth, vinegar, sugar and pepper. Cover; microwave on HIGH 5 minutes or until boiling, stirring twice during cooking.

5. Meanwhile, peel potatoes if desired; cut potatoes into cubes. Stir into broth mixture; stir in bacon. Sprinkle with parsley; serve warm. Makes about 5 cups or 8 servings.

TIP   You'll notice that microwave recipes often direct you to pierce or puncture foods with a fork or skewer. The reason for piercing is that microwaves cause steam to build up quickly in foods. Unless a food with a skin or membrane is pierced, the steam can't escape and therefore, the food may explode, making a mess in your oven. Some foods that must be pierced are whole eggs, egg yolks, potatoes and other whole vegetables.

Barley Salad

 2 tablespoons butter or margarine
 $\frac{1}{2}$ cup barley, uncooked
 $\frac{1}{2}$ cup chopped onion
 1 clove garlic, minced
 $\frac{1}{4}$ teaspoon dried thyme leaves, crushed
 1 can ($14\frac{1}{2}$ ounces) Swanson Clear Ready to Serve
    Chicken Broth
 1 medium zucchini, shredded
 $\frac{1}{2}$ cup chopped tomato
 $\frac{1}{4}$ cup chopped green onions
 2 tablespoons chopped fresh parsley
 1 tablespoon rice wine vinegar
 1 tablespoon chopped capers
 $\frac{1}{4}$ teaspoon pepper

1. In 2-quart microwave-safe casserole, combine butter, barley, onion, garlic and thyme. Cover with lid; microwave on HIGH 4 minutes or until onion is tender, stirring once during cooking.

2. Stir in broth. Cover; microwave on HIGH 5 minutes or until bubbling, stirring once during cooking. Reduce power to 50%. Microwave 25 minutes or until barley is tender and liquid is absorbed, stirring twice during cooking.

3. Cool slightly. Stir in remaining ingredients. Cover; refrigerate until serving time, at least 4 hours. Makes about 4 cups or 8 servings.

TIP   To remove food odors from the microwave oven, place a cut lemon or the part of a lemon that's left after juicing in a custard cup; microwave, uncovered, on HIGH about 1 minute.

Sauces

Onion-Cheese Sauce

Served over toast and sprinkled with cooked bacon, this sauce becomes a luscious, light supper or brunch entrée.

1 can (10³/₄ ounces) Campbell's Condensed Creamy Onion Soup/Dip
1¹/₂ cups shredded sharp Cheddar cheese (6 ounces)
¹/₂ cup milk
¹/₂ teaspoon dry mustard

In 2-quart microwave-safe casserole, stir soup until smooth. Stir in cheese, milk and mustard; mix well. Microwave, uncovered, on HIGH 4 minutes or until sauce is hot and cheese is melted, stirring twice during cooking. Serve with vegetables or potatoes. Makes about 2 cups.

Mushroom-Apricot Sauce

1 can (10¹/₂ ounces) Franco-American Mushroom Gravy
¹/₂ cup apricot preserves
2 tablespoons lemon juice
1 teaspoon Dijon-style mustard

In 4-cup glass measure, stir together all ingredients. Microwave, uncovered, on HIGH 4 minutes or until preserves are melted, stirring once during heating. Serve with ham or meat loaf. Makes about 2 cups.

ONION-CHEESE SAUCE ▶

Lemon Sauce

1 can (10¾ ounces) Campbell's Condensed Cream of
    Chicken Soup
½ cup water
1 teaspoon grated lemon peel
1 tablespoon lemon juice
¼ teaspoon dried tarragon leaves, crushed
    Dash hot pepper sauce (optional)

In 1-quart microwave-safe casserole, stir soup until smooth. Stir in remaining ingredients; mix well. Cover with lid; microwave on HIGH 4 minutes or until hot and bubbling, stirring twice during cooking. Serve with fish or vegetables. Makes about 1½ cups.

TIP Microwave oranges, lemons and limes on HIGH about 15 seconds before juicing them; the juice will be released more easily.

Curry Sauce

1 teaspoon butter or margarine
¼ cup chopped onion
1 teaspoon curry powder
1 can (10¾ ounces) Campbell's Condensed Cream of
    Chicken Soup
⅓ cup water

1. In 1-quart microwave-safe casserole, combine butter, onion and curry powder. Cover with lid; microwave on HIGH 3 minutes or until onion is tender, stirring once during cooking.

2. Stir in soup until smooth. Stir in water until blended. Cover; microwave on HIGH 3 minutes or until hot and bubbling, stirring once during cooking. Serve with chicken or rice. Makes about 1½ cups.

Bordelaise Sauce

2 tablespoons butter or margarine
1 tablespoon finely chopped onion
¼ teaspoon dried tarragon leaves, crushed
2 tablespoons all-purpose flour
1 can (10½ ounces) Campbell's Condensed Beef Broth
(Bouillon)
1 tablespoon dry red wine
1 teaspoon finely chopped fresh parsley
1 teaspoon lemon juice

1. In 1-quart microwave-safe casserole, combine butter, onion and tarragon. Cover with lid; microwave on HIGH 2 minutes or until onion is tender.

2. Stir in flour. Gradually stir in broth. Add wine, parsley and lemon juice. Cover; microwave on HIGH 4 minutes or until mixture boils, stirring twice during cooking. Serve with beef or liver. Makes about 1½ cups.

Stroganoff Sauce

1 teaspoon butter or margarine
¼ cup chopped onion
1 can (10¾ ounces) Campbell's Condensed Cream of
Mushroom Soup
⅓ cup sour cream
¼ cup milk
¼ teaspoon paprika

1. In 1-quart microwave-safe casserole, combine butter and onion. Cover with lid; microwave on HIGH 3 minutes or until onion is tender, stirring once during cooking.

2. Stir in soup until smooth. Stir in sour cream, milk and paprika until blended. Cover; microwave on HIGH 3 minutes or until heated through, stirring once during cooking. Serve with beef, rice or vegetables. Makes about 2 cups.

Madeira-Mushroom Gravy

1 tablespoon butter or margarine
1 cup sliced Campbell's Fresh Mushrooms
1 tablespoon chopped green onion
1 can (10¼ ounces) Franco-American Beef Gravy
2 tablespoons tomato paste
1 tablespoon Madeira wine
½ teaspoon chopped fresh thyme leaves or ⅛ teaspoon
dried thyme leaves, crushed

1. In 1-quart microwave-safe casserole, combine butter, mushrooms and onion. Cover with lid; microwave on HIGH 3 minutes or until mushrooms are tender, stirring once during cooking.

2. Stir in remaining ingredients. Cover; microwave on HIGH 3 minutes or until hot and bubbling. Serve with beef or pork. Makes about 2 cups.

Barbecue Sauce

1 can (11 ounces) Campbell's Condensed Zesty Tomato
Soup/Sauce
⅓ cup apricot preserves
3 tablespoons water
2 tablespoons vinegar
1 tablespoon Worcestershire sauce
1 clove garlic, minced

In 1-quart microwave-safe casserole, stir together all ingredients. Cover with lid; microwave on HIGH 5 minutes or until hot and bubbling, stirring once during cooking. Serve with hamburgers or use to baste chicken or ribs during last 10 minutes of broiling or grilling. Makes about 1½ cups.

FROM TOP TO BOTTOM: MADEIRA-MUSHROOM GRAVY,
BARBECUE SAUCE, CHILI CON QUESO SAUCE (SEE PAGE 158) ▶

Chili con Queso Sauce

**1 can (11 ounces) Campbell's Condensed Nacho Cheese
    Soup/Dip**
½ cup water
1 tablespoon chopped fresh parsley or cilantro
¼ teaspoon ground cumin
½ cup chopped tomato

In 1-quart microwave-safe casserole, stir soup until smooth. Stir in water, parsley and cumin; mix well. Microwave, uncovered, on HIGH 3 minutes or until hot and bubbling. Stir in tomato. Serve with hamburgers, potatoes or vegetables. Makes about 2 cups.

Herb Sauce

**1 can (10¾ ounces) Campbell's Condensed Cream of
    Celery Soup or Cream of Chicken Soup**
⅓ cup milk
⅛ teaspoon rubbed sage
Generous dash dried thyme leaves, crushed

In 1-quart microwave-safe casserole, stir soup until smooth. Stir in milk, sage and thyme; mix well. Cover with lid; microwave on HIGH 4 minutes or until hot and bubbling, stirring once during cooking. Serve with chicken, fish or vegetables. Makes about 1½ cups.

TIP   Glass measuring cups are perfect for microwaving sauces and other liquids; for many recipes you can measure the liquid right into the cup, then add other ingredients and heat. Handles on the measuring cups stay cool during cooking, so they're useful for transferring foods to and from the oven.

Cream Cheese Sauce

1 package (3 ounces) cream cheese, cut up
1 can (10¾ ounces) Campbell's Condensed Cream of
   Celery Soup
⅓ cup milk
¼ cup grated Parmesan cheese
   Generous dash pepper

1. Place cream cheese in 1-quart microwave-safe casserole. Microwave, uncovered, on HIGH 30 seconds or until softened.

2. Stir in soup until smooth. Stir in milk, Parmesan and pepper until well mixed. Cover with lid; microwave on HIGH 4 minutes or until hot and bubbling, stirring once during cooking. Serve with vegetables, chicken or pasta. Makes about 2 cups.

Savory Orange Sauce

2 tablespoons butter or margarine
1 tablespoon finely chopped onion
⅛ teaspoon ground ginger
1 can (10¾ ounces) Campbell's Condensed Cream of
   Mushroom Soup
1 teaspoon grated orange peel
⅓ cup orange juice

1. In 1-quart microwave-safe casserole, combine butter, onion and ginger. Cover with lid; microwave on HIGH 2 minutes or until onion is tender.

2. Stir in soup until smooth. Stir in orange peel and juice; mix well. Cover; microwave on HIGH 4 minutes or until hot and bubbling, stirring once during cooking. Serve with vegetables, duck, chicken or fish. Makes about 1½ cups.

Sauce Amandine

1 teaspoon butter or margarine
¼ cup finely chopped onion
¼ cup sliced almonds
1 can (10¾ ounces) Campbell's Condensed Cream of Mushroom Soup, Cream of Celery Soup or Cream of Chicken Soup
⅓ cup milk

1. In 1-quart microwave-safe casserole, combine butter, onion and almonds. Microwave, uncovered, on HIGH 3 minutes or until onion is tender and almonds are lightly browned, stirring once during cooking.

2. Stir in soup until smooth. Stir in milk until blended. Cover with lid; microwave on HIGH 3 minutes or until hot and bubbling, stirring once during cooking. Serve with fish, chicken or vegetables. Makes about 1½ cups.

Note: Substitute chopped pecans or walnuts for almonds.

Tomato Cream Sauce

1 teaspoon butter or margarine
¼ cup finely chopped onion
⅛ teaspoon dried thyme leaves, crushed
1 can (10¾ ounces) Campbell's Condensed Tomato Soup
½ cup sour cream
2 tablespoons water
2 teaspoons paprika

1. In 1-quart microwave-safe casserole, combine butter, onion and thyme. Cover with lid; microwave on HIGH 3 minutes or until onion is tender, stirring once during cooking.

2. Stir in soup, sour cream, water and paprika until smooth. Cover; microwave on HIGH 3 minutes or until heated through, stirring once during cooking. Serve with hamburgers, pasta, chicken or vegetables. Makes about 2 cups.

Fresh Mushroom Sauce

3 tablespoons butter or margarine
3 tablespoons all-purpose flour
1 can (10¾ ounces) Campbell's Condensed Chicken
     Broth
¼ cup water
 1 tablespoon lemon juice
 1 tablespoon dry vermouth
1½ cups sliced Campbell's Fresh Mushrooms
 2 tablespoons chopped fresh parsley

1. Place butter in 4-cup glass measure. Cover; microwave on HIGH 40 seconds or until melted.

2. Stir in flour until smooth. Stir in broth, water, lemon juice and vermouth. Microwave, uncovered, on HIGH 5 minutes or until boiling, stirring once during cooking.

3. Stir in mushrooms and parsley. Microwave, uncovered, on HIGH 3 minutes or until just boiling, stirring once during cooking. Serve with chicken or fish. Makes about 2½ cups.

Note: Slice mushrooms using a hard-cooked egg slicer for uniform pieces in record time.

TIP   New on the market are microwave-safe plastic spoons and whisks. They're especially handy for use with recipes that require frequent stirring; you can leave the spoon or whisk right in the container during microwaving.

Just for Kids

Chili Dogs

1 can (11¼ ounces) Campbell's Condensed Chili Beef Soup
2 tablespoons water
2 tablespoons ketchup
6 frankfurters
6 Pepperidge Farm Frankfurter Rolls, split
3 slices American cheese, cut into triangles

1. In small microwave-safe bowl, combine soup, water and ketchup. Cover with vented plastic wrap; microwave on HIGH 3 minutes or until very hot, stirring once during cooking.

2. Arrange frankfurters on 10-inch microwave-safe plate lined with paper towels. Microwave, uncovered, on HIGH 2 minutes or until hot.

3. Place cooked frankfurters in rolls. Spoon a heaping tablespoon of soup mixture over each. Arrange cheese triangles over soup mixture.

4. Arrange rolls on same plate lined with clean paper towels. Microwave, uncovered, on HIGH 1 minute or until cheese melts. Makes 6 servings.

CHILI DOGS, ENGLISH MUFFIN
PIZZAS, (SEE PAGE 164) ▶

English Muffin Pizzas

2 English muffins, split and toasted
¼ cup Prego Spaghetti Sauce
¼ cup shredded mozzarella cheese (1 ounce)
  Pepperoni or frankfurter slices for garnish
  Sliced olives, green pepper or mushrooms for garnish

1. Spread each muffin half with 1 tablespoon spaghetti sauce; sprinkle with 1 tablespoon cheese. Top with garnish, if desired.

2. Arrange pizzas in circular pattern on microwave-safe plate lined with paper towels. Microwave, uncovered, on HIGH 1½ minutes or until cheese melts, rotating plate once during cooking. Makes 4 pizzas.

Souper Sandwiches

1 pound ground beef
1 can (11 ounces) Campbell's Condensed Zesty Tomato
   Soup/Sauce
4 Pepperidge Farm French-Style Rolls, split
½ cup shredded mozzarella cheese (2 ounces)

1. Crumble beef into 1½-quart microwave-safe casserole. Cover with lid; microwave on HIGH 5 minutes or until beef is no longer pink, stirring once during cooking to break up meat. Spoon off fat.

2. Stir in soup. Cover; microwave on HIGH 3 minutes or until hot and bubbling, stirring once during cooking.

3. Arrange bottom halves of 2 rolls on 10-inch microwave-safe plate lined with paper towels. Spread ½ cup of the meat mixture over each; sprinkle each with ¼ of the cheese. Microwave, uncovered, on HIGH 1 minute or until cheese is melted; cover with top halves of rolls. Repeat with remaining ingredients. Makes 4 servings.

Note: You can also use this filling in taco shells or spoon it onto hamburger buns.

Just-for-Two Lasagna

Of course, this isn't really lasagna, but it tastes like lasagna and takes just 20 easy minutes from start to finish.

1 can (15 ounces) Franco-American Beef RavioliOs in Meat Sauce
1 egg
½ cup ricotta cheese
1 tablespoon chopped fresh parsley
½ cup shredded mozzarella cheese (2 ounces)
2 tablespoons grated Parmesan cheese

1. Divide RavioliOs between two 12-ounce microwave-safe casseroles.

2. In small bowl, beat egg; stir in ricotta and parsley. Spoon over RavioliOs. Sprinkle with mozzarella and Parmesan. Microwave, uncovered, at 50% power 10 minutes or until heated through, rearranging dishes once during cooking. Let stand, uncovered, 5 minutes. Makes 2 servings.

TIP Kids take to microwave ovens lots faster than adults who have preconceived notions of cooking. Many parents prefer that their children use microwave ovens rather than conventional ranges, as they will not be exposed to hot burners and ovens. But there are a few precautions that children should know before using the appliance.
• Don't operate the microwave oven when it is empty.
• Use hot pads to remove food from the microwave oven and to rotate dishes—they can become hot.
• Check foods before tasting—food may be hotter than it looks.
• Be extra careful when removing a cover from food that has been microwaved—steam from the food can burn you.
• If a recipe has a standing time, be patient. Standing time is important to complete cooking.
• Clean up spills in the oven and on the door seals as soon as they happen.

Macaroni and Cheese

1 can (11 ounces) Campbell's Condensed Cheddar
    Cheese Soup/Sauce
3/4 cup milk
  2 cups shredded Cheddar cheese (8 ounces)
1/2 teaspoon prepared mustard
    Dash pepper
  3 cups cooked elbow macaroni (1 1/2 cups uncooked)

1. In 2-quart microwave-safe casserole, stir soup until smooth; gradually stir in milk until blended. Stir in cheese, mustard and pepper. Stir in macaroni.

2. Cover with lid; microwave on HIGH 10 minutes or until hot and bubbling, stirring twice during cooking. Let stand, covered, 5 minutes. Makes 5 cups or 5 servings.

TIP To make an upside-down hot fudge sundae: Place 1 or 2 tablespoons fudge sauce in a microwave-safe serving dish. Microwave on HIGH 10 seconds or until hot. Top with ice cream, nuts and other sundae favorites.

Chocolate Pretzel Crunch

1 package (12 ounces) semisweet chocolate pieces
1 tablespoon shortening
1 bag (5 1/2 ounces) Pepperidge Farm Pretzel Goldfish
    Crackers
1 cup unsalted peanuts

1. In large microwave-safe bowl, combine chocolate pieces and shortening. Microwave, uncovered, on HIGH 2 minutes or until melted, stirring once during cooking.

2. Stir in pretzels and peanuts until well mixed. Drop by teaspoonfuls onto baking sheets lined with waxed paper. Refrigerate until firm; store in refrigerator. Makes about 45 pieces.

Note: Substitute 1 package (12 ounces) butterscotch-flavored pieces for the chocolate.

CHOCOLATE PRETZEL CRUNCH ▶

Breads and Sweets

Carrot-Bran Muffins

¾ cup "V8" Vegetable Juice
1 cup bran cereal flakes
1½ cups finely shredded carrots
¼ cup raisins
1 egg, beaten
2 tablespoons vegetable oil
¼ cup packed brown sugar
1 cup all-purpose flour
1 teaspoon baking powder
½ teaspoon baking soda
½ teaspoon ground cinnamon
¼ teaspoon ground nutmeg

1. In medium bowl, combine "V8" juice, cereal, carrots and raisins; let stand 5 minutes. Add remaining ingredients; stir until just mixed.

2. Place 2 paper liners in each cup of microwave-safe muffin ring or 6 custard cups. Fill cups ½ full with batter. Microwave, 6 at a time, uncovered, on HIGH 2½ minutes or until toothpick inserted in center comes out clean, rotating or rearranging once during cooking.

3. Repeat step 2 with remaining batter. Makes 12 muffins.

CARROT-BRAN MUFFINS ▶

Nacho Corn Bread

1 cup plus 1 tablespoon yellow cornmeal
1 cup all-purpose flour
¼ cup sugar
1 tablespoon baking powder
1 can (11 ounces) Campbell's Condensed Nacho Cheese
    Soup/Dip
1 egg, beaten
½ cup milk
1 tablespoon vegetable oil
½ cup chopped onion

1. Grease 9-inch microwave-safe ring pan. Dust with 1 tablespoon cornmeal.

2. In medium bowl, combine 1 cup cornmeal, flour, sugar and baking powder.

3. In small bowl, stir soup until smooth. Add egg, milk, oil and onion; stir until well blended. Pour all at once into dry ingredients; stir just until flour is moistened (batter will be stiff).

4. Spread evenly in prepared pan. Microwave, uncovered, at 50% power 6 minutes, rotating pan once during cooking.

5. Increase power to HIGH. Microwave, uncovered, 4 minutes or until toothpick inserted in bread comes out clean, rotating pan once during cooking. Let stand directly on countertop 5 minutes. Invert onto serving plate. Makes 8 servings.

TIP   Use the microwave to defrost frozen bread dough in a fraction of the time. Follow package directions or simply microwave at 50% or lower power, checking frequently.

Coconut-Pecan Coffeecake

¼ cup butter or margarine
⅓ cup sugar
1 egg
½ teaspoon vanilla extract
¾ cup sour cream
1 cup all-purpose flour
1½ teaspoons baking powder
1 package (5¾ ounces) Pepperidge Farm Date Pecan
    Cookies, finely crushed
½ cup flaked coconut

1. Lightly grease 8-inch round microwave-safe baking dish; set aside. Place butter in large microwave-safe bowl. Microwave, uncovered, on HIGH 15 seconds or until softened. Beat in sugar, egg and vanilla until smooth. Beat in sour cream. Fold in flour, baking powder and ½ cup of the cookie crumbs until well mixed.

2. Spread batter evenly in prepared dish. Sprinkle remaining cookie crumbs and coconut over batter. Microwave, uncovered, at 50% power 6 minutes, rotating dish once during cooking.

3. Increase power to HIGH. Microwave, uncovered, 2½ minutes or until toothpick inserted in center comes out clean, rotating dish once during cooking. Let stand directly on countertop 10 minutes. Makes 8 servings.

Note: Crush cookies in blender or food processor.

TIP   To soften butter for easier spreading, place ½ cup butter on microwave-safe plate. Microwave on HIGH 10 seconds.

Tomato Soup Spice Cake

This version of our classic spice cake comes out even higher and lighter than the version baked in the conventional oven.

1 tablespoon sugar
1 box (about 18 ounces) spice cake mix
1 can (10¾ ounces) Campbell's Condensed Tomato Soup
2 eggs
2 tablespoons water
1 cup sour cream
¼ cup packed brown sugar
1 teaspoon vanilla extract

1. Generously grease 14-cup microwave-safe Bundt® pan. Sprinkle pan with sugar.

2. In large bowl, combine cake mix, soup, eggs and water. With mixer, beat 2 minutes or until well mixed, constantly scraping side and bottom of bowl.

3. Pour into prepared pan. Microwave, uncovered, at 50% power 9 minutes, rotating pan once during cooking.

4. Increase power to HIGH. Microwave, uncovered, 5 minutes or until toothpick inserted into cake comes out clean. Let stand directly on countertop 15 minutes. Invert onto serving plate; cool completely.

5. In small bowl, stir together sour cream, brown sugar and vanilla until sugar dissolves. Spoon evenly over cooled cake. Makes 12 servings.

TIP   On a cold winter night, warm up with Hot Buttered "V8". Pour ¾ cup "V8" Vegetable Juice into a microwave-safe mug; add 1 teaspoon butter. Microwave on HIGH 1½ minutes.

TOMATO SOUP SPICE CAKE ▶

Amaretti Cupcakes

*Look for Lazzaroni Amaretti Biscuits at gourmet shops and
department stores.*

¼ cup butter or margarine, softened
½ cup sugar
1 egg
½ cup milk
1 teaspoon vanilla extract
1 cup all-purpose flour
1 teaspoon baking powder
**1 cup (12 pairs) finely crushed Lazzaroni Amaretti di
    Saronno Biscuits**
1 teaspoon ground cinnamon
3 tablespoons butter or margarine

1. In medium bowl, beat ¼ cup butter and sugar until smooth. Beat in egg,
milk and vanilla. Fold in flour, baking powder and ½ cup of the biscuit
crumbs.

2. Place 2 paper liners in each cup of microwave-safe muffin ring or 6
custard cups. Fill cups ½ full with batter. Microwave, 6 at a time, uncovered,
on HIGH 2½ minutes or until toothpick inserted in center comes out clean,
rotating or rearranging once during cooking. Repeat step 2 with remaining
batter.

3. In small bowl, combine remaining ½ cup crumbs and cinnamon. Place 3
tablespoons butter in small microwave-safe bowl. Cover; microwave on HIGH
40 seconds or until melted. Dip top of each cupcake into butter, then into
crumb mixture. Makes 12 cupcakes.

TIP   For a quick snack, warm a muffin, doughnut or soft
pretzel in the microwave oven on a paper towel. Microwave on
HIGH 10 to 20 seconds to bring back that just-baked flavor.

Fudgy Cookie Brownies

Cut these rich brownies into thin wedges, then top with ice cream for a truly special dessert.

6 tablespoons butter or margarine, cut up
2 squares (1 ounce each) unsweetened chocolate
1 cup sugar
1 teaspoon vanilla extract
2 eggs
1/2 cup all-purpose flour
1/2 teaspoon baking powder
1 cup coarsely crushed Pepperidge Farm Chocolate Chunk Pecan, Chocolate Chocolate Chip or Peanut Butter Chip Cookies

1. In large microwave-safe bowl, place butter and chocolate. Microwave, uncovered, at 50% power 2½ minutes or until chocolate is melted, stirring twice during heating.

2. Stir in sugar and vanilla. Add eggs, one at a time, beating well after each addition. Stir in flour and baking powder. Fold in cookies.

3. Spread batter in 8-inch round microwave-safe baking dish. Elevate if necessary (see page 7). Microwave, uncovered, at 50% power 8 minutes or until edges appear dry but center is still wet, rotating dish once during cooking.

4. Increase power to HIGH. Microwave, uncovered, 2 minutes or until toothpick inserted in center comes out clean, rotating dish once during cooking. Let stand directly on countertop until cool before cutting. Makes 16 brownies.

Note: Be sure to stir chocolate during melting; chocolate holds its shape during melting and could burn while it still looks solid.

TIP To melt chocolate, place 1 square (1 ounce) unsweetened chocolate in a microwave-safe dish. Microwave, uncovered, at 50% power 1½ minutes. Chocolate tends to hold its shape even when melted, so stir to check before adding more time.

Trifle

1 Pepperidge Farm Frozen All Butter Pound Cake
    (10¾ ounces)
¼ cup raspberry preserves
¼ cup sugar
1 tablespoon cornstarch
2½ cups milk
3 eggs
2 teaspoons vanilla extract
¼ cup cream sherry
1 can (16 ounces) sliced peaches, drained, or 2 cups
    sliced fresh peaches (optional)
1 cup heavy cream, whipped

1. Slice cake horizontally into 3 layers. Spread preserves between layers. Reassemble layers and cut into bite-size pieces; set aside.

2. In 4-cup glass measure, stir together sugar and cornstarch; stir in milk. Microwave, uncovered, on HIGH 6½ minutes or until bubbling, stirring twice during cooking.

3. In small bowl, beat eggs until foamy. Add ½ cup of the hot milk mixture to eggs, stirring constantly. Return egg mixture to hot milk, stirring constantly. Microwave, uncovered, on HIGH 30 seconds or until slightly thickened, stirring once during cooking. Stir in vanilla.

4. Arrange ½ of the cake pieces in 2-quart bowl. Sprinkle with ½ of the sherry. Top with ½ of the peaches, then ½ of the custard. Repeat layers with remaining cake, sherry, peaches and custard. Cover; refrigerate at least 4 hours.

5. Just before serving, garnish with whipped cream. Makes 8 servings.

Note: If frozen cake is too firm to slice, microwave on HIGH 1 minute; let stand 3 minutes.

TIP Use your microwave oven to warm small quantities of brandy or other liquor for flaming. Pour 2 tablespoons into a glass measure or custard cup. Microwave, uncovered, on HIGH 15 seconds; *do not boil*. Remove from microwave oven. Pour liquor over food and carefully ignite with a long match.

Cinnamon-Raisin Bread Pudding

4 cups cubed Pepperidge Farm Cinnamon Bread
¹/₂ cup raisins
1¹/₂ cups milk
2 eggs, beaten
¹/₂ cup packed brown sugar
1 tablespoon brandy (optional)
¹/₂ teaspoon ground nutmeg
Brandied Sauce (recipe follows)

1. In 1¹/₂-quart microwave-safe casserole, toss together bread cubes and raisins; set aside.

2. Pour milk into 4-cup glass measure. Microwave, uncovered, on HIGH 2 minutes or until warm. Stir eggs, brown sugar, brandy and nutmeg into milk until sugar dissolves.

3. Microwave, uncovered, at 50% power 2 minutes or until heated through. Pour over bread cubes.

4. Cover with waxed paper; microwave at 50% power 8 minutes or until custard is set, rotating dish every 2 minutes. Let stand 5 minutes. Serve with Brandied Sauce. Makes 6 servings.

Note: Substitute Pepperidge Farm Raisin Bread for cinnamon bread and omit raisins.

Brandied Sauce: In 2-cup glass measure, combine ¼ cup butter or margarine, ¹/₂ cup packed brown sugar, 3 tablespoons brandy and ¹/₈ teaspoon ground nutmeg. Microwave, uncovered, on HIGH 2¹/₂ minutes or until hot and bubbling, stirring twice during cooking.

TIP For the aroma of fresh-baked goodies, combine ¹/₂ cup water with some cinnamon, cloves and other spices in a microwave-safe bowl. Microwave, uncovered, on HIGH until boiling, then set the bowl out to scent the room. Or, substitute 2 teaspoons vanilla extract for the spices.

Cheesecake Pie

6 tablespoons butter or margarine
1½ cups graham cracker crumbs
2 packages (8 ounces each) cream cheese
1 can (11 ounces) Campbell's Condensed Cheddar Cheese Soup/Sauce
3 eggs
½ cup sugar
2 teaspoons grated lemon peel
2 tablespoons lemon juice
1 teaspoon vanilla extract
½ cup sour cream
Chocolate Leaves for garnish (recipe follows)
Fruit for garnish

1. To make crust: Place butter in 10-inch microwave-safe pie plate. Cover; microwave on HIGH 45 seconds or until melted. Stir in crumbs; mix well. Press mixture on bottom and side of pie plate. Microwave, uncovered, on HIGH 1½ minutes, rotating plate once during cooking. Set aside.

2. To make filling: Place cream cheese in large microwave-safe bowl. Microwave, uncovered, on HIGH 1 minute or until softened. With electric mixer, beat cream cheese until smooth. Add soup, eggs, sugar, lemon peel, lemon juice and vanilla; beat until smooth. Microwave, uncovered, on HIGH 7 minutes or until mixture is hot and very thick, stirring often during cooking.

3. Pour filling into prepared crust. Microwave, uncovered, at 50% power 5 minutes or until almost set in center, rotating dish once during cooking. Let stand directly on countertop until completely cool. Refrigerate until serving time, at least 4 hours.

4. Spread sour cream evenly over cheesecake. Garnish with Chocolate Leaves and fruit. Makes 12 servings.

Chocolate Leaves: In small microwave-safe bowl, combine 2 squares (1 ounce each) semisweet chocolate and 1 teaspoon shortening. Microwave, uncovered, at 50% power 2½ minutes or until chocolate is melted, stirring twice during heating. Brush a thin layer of melted chocolate on veined side of a nontoxic leaf such as an orange or rose leaf. Place chocolate-side up on cookie sheet lined with waxed paper. Refrigerate until chocolate is firm, then carefully peel chocolate from leaf.

Or, spread melted chocolate in a thin layer on waxed paper and refrigerate until firm but not hard. Use a sharp knife or cookie cutters to cut leaves or other decorative shapes.

CHEESECAKE PIE ▶

Fruit Crumble

Increase the amount of lemon juice when using sweeter apples.

4 cups thinly sliced peeled apples
¼ cup packed brown sugar
1 teaspoon lemon juice
¼ teaspoon ground cinnamon
2 tablespoons butter or margarine
½ package (5- to 8-ounce size) Pepperidge Farm Irish Oatmeal, Hazelnut or Lemon Nut Cookies, coarsely crushed (about 1 cup)
½ cup chopped walnuts (optional)

1. In large bowl, toss together apples, brown sugar, lemon juice and cinnamon. Spoon mixture into 9-inch microwave-safe pie plate; set aside.

2. Place butter in medium microwave-safe bowl. Cover; microwave on HIGH 30 seconds or until melted. Stir in cookies and walnuts. Sprinkle over apple mixture.

3. Microwave, uncovered, on HIGH 7 minutes or until apples are tender, rotating dish twice during cooking. Let stand, uncovered, 5 minutes. Makes 6 servings.

Note: Substitute a 21-ounce can of apple or cherry pie filling for fresh apples. Omit brown sugar. Microwave as directed above.

TIP To soften brown sugar, place 1 pound brown sugar in a microwave-safe container. Cover; microwave on HIGH 30 seconds.

Almond-Crumb Peaches

8 Pepperidge Farm Almond Supreme Cookies, finely crushed
2 tablespoons almond-flavored liqueur
4 ripe peaches, halved and pitted
Whipped cream for garnish

1. In small bowl, stir together cookies and liqueur.

2. Arrange peaches, cut-side up, in circular pattern on 10-inch microwave-safe plate. Spoon some of the cookie mixture into center of each peach. Microwave, uncovered, on HIGH 4 minutes or until peaches are tender, rotating dish once during cooking. Garnish with whipped cream. Makes 4 servings.

Note: Substitute 8 canned peach halves, drained, for fresh peaches. Reduce cooking time to 2 minutes or until peaches are heated through.

Cookie Ice Cream Supreme

½ gallon vanilla ice cream
1 package (6½ ounces) Pepperidge Farm Capri Brownie Creme Cookies, coarsely crushed
½ cup raspberry preserves
1 tablespoon lemon juice
1 tablespoon orange-flavored liqueur

1. Place ice cream in large microwave-safe bowl. Microwave, uncovered, at 50% power 2 minutes or until softened, stirring once during heating.

2. Stir in cookies until well blended. Spoon into 10-inch pie plate. Cover; freeze 3 hours or until firm.

3. Just before serving, prepare sauce. In small microwave-safe bowl, stir together preserves, lemon juice and liqueur. Microwave, uncovered, on HIGH 1½ minutes or until preserves are melted, stirring once during heating.

4. To serve, let ice cream stand at room temperature 5 minutes; cut into wedges. Serve with warm sauce. Makes 10 servings.

TIP   Soften very hard ice cream right in the carton. Microwave on HIGH, checking every 15 seconds.

Frozen Food Guide

FROZEN PREPARED FOODS AND YOUR MICROWAVE OVEN

With today's busy schedules, the frozen food case can be a meal planner's best friend. It can provide you with quick and delicious no-work meals. And, it can rescue you when you're too tired to cook, when unexpected company drops by or when your kids need to fix a quick meal.

Keeping a supply of your favorite frozen foods on hand is good meal management. Your microwave oven makes these dishes doubly attractive, since it can heat them in a fraction of the conventional cooking time.

To make cooking and eating frozen prepared foods even more of a pleasure, read through the following ideas. The chapter ends with a collection of tips that will guarantee your frozen foods emerge from the microwave oven perfectly done.

Unbeatable Breakfasts

Everyone in your family can have his favorite breakfast whenever he rolls out of bed. Just point him toward the freezer for a Great Starts breakfast or breakfast sandwich from Swanson, then to the microwave oven for some quick cooking. To round out the meal, try one of these:

Specialty toast: Spread toast with butter, then top with a mixture of sugar and cocoa or sugar and ground cinnamon; enjoy with eggs.

Breakfast drink: In a blender, mix milk or buttermilk with fresh fruit (strawberries, banana, peach slices) and honey to taste. Blend until frothy and serve with a breakfast sandwich.

Yogurt sundae: Top plain or vanilla yogurt with berries or sliced bananas or peaches, then sprinkle with granola to go along with scrambled eggs or an omelet.

French toast and pancake toppers: Choose one of these scrumptious, last-minute complements for French toast or pancakes:

Applesauced Pancakes

1 package (6 ounces) Great Starts Frozen Pancakes with Sausages
¼ cup applesauce
1 tablespoon shredded coconut

1. Prepare pancakes with sausages according to package directions.

2. Place applesauce in small microwave-safe bowl. Microwave, uncovered, on HIGH 30 seconds or until just warm. Spoon applesauce over pancakes; sprinkle with coconut. Makes 1 serving.

Spiked Pancakes and Sausages

Substitute your own favorite jam or jelly for the marmalade.

1 package (6 ounces) Great Starts Frozen Pancakes with Sausages
2 tablespoons orange marmalade
1 tablespoon orange-flavored liqueur

1. Prepare pancakes according to package directions.

2. In small microwave-safe bowl, combine marmalade and liqueur. Microwave, uncovered, on HIGH 30 seconds or until marmalade is melted. Pour over pancakes. Makes 1 serving.

Peach Melba Pancakes

This topper also complements Great Starts Cinnamon Swirl French Toast.

1 package (6 ounces) Great Starts Frozen Pancakes with Sausages
1 tablespoon raspberry preserves
1 teaspoon water
3 fresh or canned peach slices

1. Prepare pancakes with sausages according to package directions.

2. In microwave-safe custard cup, stir together preserves and water. Microwave, uncovered, on HIGH 30 seconds or until hot. Arrange peach slices over hot pancakes; top with raspberry mixture. Makes 1 serving.

Cheesecake-Topped Pancakes

1 package (7 ounces) Great Starts Frozen Pancakes & Blueberries in Sauce or Pancakes & Strawberries in Sauce
1 ounce cream cheese
1 tablespoon milk
1 teaspoon sugar

1. Prepare pancakes according to package directions.

2. Place cream cheese in small microwave-safe bowl. Microwave, uncovered, on HIGH 15 seconds or until softened. Stir in milk and sugar until smooth.

3. Stir hot berry topping into cream cheese mixture; pour over pancakes. Makes 1 serving.

PEACH MELBA PANCAKES ▶

French Toast Deluxe

1 package (6½ ounces) Great Starts Frozen Cinnamon
   Swirl French Toast with Sausages
2 tablespoons maple-flavored syrup
1 tablespoon chopped walnuts or pecans
1 tablespoon raisins

1. Prepare French toast with sausages according to package directions.

2. In small microwave-safe bowl, stir together syrup, nuts and raisins. Microwave, uncovered, on HIGH 30 seconds or until hot. Pour warm syrup mixture over French toast. Makes 1 serving.

TIP   Warm chilled or room-temperature syrup right in a microwave-safe pitcher. Microwave on HIGH about 1 minute for ½ cup syrup.

Dinner for One or Two

Eating alone or with a companion can be satisfying if you treat yourselves like company. Choose from any number of Swanson and Le Menu frozen dinners and entrées, then cook according to package directions. Meanwhile, set the table with linens and flowers. If you like, choose one of the following additions to make your meal extra special:

Swanson Chicken Duets Entrées: These luscious stuffed chicken portions were made for the two of you. Heat according to package microwave directions, then drizzle with microwave-melted apple jelly for a shiny finish.

Vegetable salad: Nothing says freshness like a crisp vegetable salad. Simply toss some shredded lettuce with your favorite dressing, or add cherry tomatoes, cucumber slices, green pepper strips or shredded carrot for color and flavor.

Tomato and cucumber salad: Top sliced tomato and cucumber with a favorite salad dressing or herbed vinegar.

Guacamole salad: Mash a ripe avocado half with garlic, salt and chili powder to taste; spoon over shredded lettuce and tomato wedges.

Creamy cucumbers: Thinly slice cucumbers, then fold in sour cream or yogurt and fresh or dried dill, tarragon or parsley.

Marinated vegetables: Pour bottled vinaigrette or Italian salad dressing over leftover cooked green beans, broccoli, cauliflower, carrots or peas. Add fresh sweet red pepper strips or celery slices for extra crunch.

Candied sweet potatoes: Who says you need a crowd or a holiday to have sweet potatoes? Mrs. Paul's Frozen Sweet Potatoes can be ready in minutes any day of the year.

Ambrosia: For a salad or dessert, combine sliced orange and crushed pineapple; garnish with flaked coconut and maraschino cherries.

Warmed grapefruit: Sprinkle cut edge of 2 grapefruit halves with brown sugar and cinnamon. Place on microwave-safe plates. Microwave, uncovered, on HIGH 3 minutes or until warm.

Ice cream sundae: A scoop of ice cream drizzled with your favorite liqueur or ice cream topping will leave no doubt that you've had a wonderful meal.

Berries supreme: Spoon strawberries, blueberries or raspberries into a dessert dish; top with a dollop of sour cream or yogurt and a sprinkling of brown sugar.

Microwave desserts: For a satisfying end to your meal, prepare one of these quick-and-easy desserts for one or two servings:

Poached Pears

1 large ripe pear, peeled
2 tablespoons Port wine or crème de menthe

1. Cut pear in half; scoop out core and seeds. Arrange both halves in 1-quart microwave-safe casserole. Spoon 1 tablespoon wine over each half.

2. Cover with lid; microwave on HIGH 3 minutes or until pear is tender. Let stand, covered, 5 minutes. Spoon liquid over pears before serving. Makes 2 servings.

Fruit and Pudding

Serve this creamy pudding over bananas, peaches, strawberries, blueberries or cherries.

2 tablespoons sugar
1½ teaspoons cornstarch
½ cup milk
1 egg, beaten
½ teaspoon vanilla extract
1 cup sliced fruit

1. In 2-cup glass measure, stir together sugar and cornstarch. Gradually stir in milk and egg until smooth. Microwave, uncovered, on HIGH 2 minutes or until boiling, stirring twice during cooking. Stir in vanilla.

2. Divide fruit between 2 dessert bowls. Pour warm pudding over fruit. Makes about 1 cup pudding or 2 servings.

Apple Crisp for One

This quick dessert can also be made with a large peach.

1 tablespoon butter or margarine
2 tablespoons dark brown sugar
2 tablespoons quick-cooking oats
1 tablespoon all-purpose flour
⅛ teaspoon ground cinnamon
1 medium apple, peeled and sliced
Whipped cream or ice cream for garnish

1. Place butter in 1-cup glass measure. Microwave, uncovered, on HIGH 10 seconds or until softened. Stir in sugar, oats, flour and cinnamon; set aside.

2. Place apple slices in small microwave-safe bowl. Sprinkle oat mixture over apple. Microwave, uncovered, on HIGH 2½ minutes or until apple is tender, rotating dish once during cooking. Serve warm or chilled; garnish with whipped cream. Makes 1 serving.

Party Presto

When unexpected guests descend on you, be prepared with a freezer full of party food. Leave the cooking to your microwave oven, and spend those precious last minutes readying your home or yourself. Below are some examples of festive morsels and serving suggestions.

Mini-pizzas: To make attractive hors d'oeuvres, simply prepare Pepperidge Farm Croissant Pastry Pizzas according to package microwave directions, then cut into bite-size pieces.

Chicken Duets: These stuffed gourmet chicken nuggets need no further embellishment. Microwave your favorite variety and serve plain. Or spear each on a cocktail pick with a stuffed olive, a roasted red pepper square or a cherry tomato half.

Chicken bites: Prepare your favorite Swanson Frozen Chicken Dipsters or Nibbles. Serve with a prepared sweet-and-sour sauce or whip up one of these delicious sauces: Oriental Dipping Sauce, Sweet Relish Sauce or Sweet and Spunky Dip. (Recipes follow.)

Fish fry: Mrs. Paul's Frozen Crispy Crunchy Fish Fillets are even more delicious and attractive with a simple garnish of layered orange, lime and lemon slices.

Picnic chicken: Microwave Swanson Plump & Juicy Fried Chicken (pick your favorite parts), then serve in a basket lined with a colorful napkin. Accompany with cole slaw, potato salad and lemonade.

Glazed chicken: Honey-Mustard Chicken using Swanson's Frozen Fried Chicken makes an easy but mouth-watering Sunday dinner. No one will ever guess the chicken was frozen just minutes ago. (Recipe follows.)

Honey-Mustard Chicken

**1 package (32 ounces) Swanson Frozen Plump & Juicy
   Fried Chicken
1 tablespoon butter or margarine
¼ cup finely chopped green onions
3 tablespoons honey
1 teaspoon Dijon-style mustard**

1. Prepare chicken according to package directions.

2. To make glaze: In small microwave-safe bowl, combine butter and onions. Cover with vented plastic wrap; microwave on HIGH 2 minutes or until onions are tender.

3. Stir in honey and mustard. Microwave, uncovered, on HIGH 1 minute or until hot. Drizzle glaze over chicken. Makes 6 servings.

Sweet and Spunky Dip

**1 can (8 ounces) crushed pineapple in juice, undrained
½ cup apricot preserves
1 tablespoon soy sauce
2 teaspoons Louisiana-style hot sauce
¼ teaspoon dry mustard**

1. Place pineapple with its juice in blender or food processor. Cover; blend until smooth. Pour into 2-cup glass measure.

2. Stir in remaining ingredients. Microwave, uncovered, on HIGH 3 minutes or until bubbling, stirring once during cooking.

3. Serve warm with Swanson Chicken Dipsters or Nibbles for dipping. Makes about 1½ cups sauce.

HONEY-MUSTARD CHICKEN ▶

Oriental Dipping Sauce

This sauce is great to use for dipping with Swanson Frozen Chicken Dipsters, Mrs. Paul's fish sticks, fried eggplant, zucchini sticks or onion rings.

  ¾ cup "V8" Vegetable Juice
  ¼ cup packed light brown sugar
  2 tablespoons rice wine vinegar or dry sherry
  1 tablespoon soy sauce
  1 tablespoon cornstarch
  ¼ teaspoon grated fresh ginger

1. In medium microwave-safe bowl, stir together all ingredients. Cover with waxed paper; microwave on HIGH 3 minutes or until hot and bubbling, stirring once during cooking.

2. Serve warm with chicken, fish or vegetables for dipping. Makes 1 cup sauce.

TIP For best results in the least time, microwave frozen breaded fish or chicken until done, then crisp in the toaster oven or broiler for a few minutes. You'll save time without giving up any quality.

Sweet Relish Sauce

  ½ cup honey
  ¼ cup Vlasic Sweet Pickle Relish
  ¼ cup Dijon-style mustard
  2 tablespoons butter or margarine
  2 tablespoons lemon juice
  2 teaspoons cornstarch

1. In 2-cup glass measure, stir together all ingredients. Microwave, uncovered, on HIGH 3 minutes or until bubbling, stirring once during cooking.

2. Serve warm with Swanson Chicken Dipsters or Nibbles for dipping. Makes about 1¼ cups sauce.

ORIENTAL DIPPING SAUCE ▶

NOTES ON MICROWAVING FROZEN FOODS

Frozen foods are among the most helpful time-savers for busy people, but there are some special things to remember when using them in your microwave oven. Be sure to read and follow the directions on frozen food packages because microwave directions for frozen dinners vary quite a bit. Even within the same dinner, one component may be piping hot before another is even thawed. That's because freezing food increases the variables that affect its microwave heating.

These different heating characteristics have been the subject of a great deal of research at Campbell Soup Company, and the research has been translated into dinners that microwave with better results. In our Creative Food Center, home economists test each dinner dozens of times in microwave ovens of various brands and wattages to develop package directions that will work in your kitchen. Package directions are based on results from 650- to 700-watt ovens.

Here are a few notes that our testers have found to be helpful in heating frozen foods:

The most important factors that affect the overall heating time are the wattage of your microwave oven and the starting temperature of the food. Heating directions are based on foods that are between 5° and 10°F., the temperature of a typical home freezer. If ice cream stays soft in your freezer, chances are it's much warmer so your frozen food will cook more quickly. On the other hand, if your deep freezer is colder than 0°F., your frozen foods may take longer to cook.

Placement of the frozen food container in the oven cavity can affect the way it cooks. Some people find that elevating the container on an inverted glass pie plate improves the evenness of heating, while other ovens heat more evenly with the container placed on the oven floor.

As a rule, cook only one frozen dinner at a time in your microwave oven. Otherwise each dinner will interfere with the cooking of the other. Instead, heat the one that requires the longer cooking time first, then heat the second. If the first has cooled a bit, return it to the microwave oven for a minute's extra heating. However, if you are cooking two identical dinners and directions are given for cooking both at once, then you'll have good results heating them together.

When thawing frozen foods (such as ground beef or meats), use a low power setting for the best results. Higher settings may cause parts of the food to begin cooking before the center has thawed. Consult your use-and-care manual for your manufacturer's recommendations.

Index